FUNA FOOD FROM AFRICA

FUNA

Renata Coetzee

FOOD FROM AFRICA

Roots of traditional
African food culture

BUTTERWORTHS
Durban / Pretoria

BUTTERWORTH & CO. (SA) (PTY) LTD
© 1982

ISBN: 0 409 10300 4
       0 409 10301 2 (De luxe)

THE BUTTERWORTH GROUP

South Africa
BUTTERWORTH & CO. (SA) (PTY) LTD
Walter Place, Waterval Park, Mayville, Durban 4091

England
BUTTERWORTH & CO. (PUBLISHERS) LTD
88 Kingsway, London WC2B 6AB

Australia
BUTTERWORTHS (PTY) LTD
PO Box 345, North Ryde, NSW 2113

Canada
BUTTERWORTH & CO. (CANADA) LTD
2265 Midland Avenue, Scarborough, Ontario MIP 4S1

New Zealand
BUTTERWORTHS OF NEW ZEALAND LTD
31–35 Cumberland Place, Wellington

USA
BUTTERWORTHS (PUBLISHERS) INC.
10 Tower Office Park, Woburn, Massachusetts 01801

Set 10 on 12pt Palatino by
Dieter Zimmermann (Pty) Ltd, Johannesburg
Photographs by Volker Miros (1, 4, 8, 11, 12) and
Günther Komnick (2, 3, 5, 6, 7, 9, 10, 13, 14, 15, 16, 17, 18, 19, 20)
Printed and bound by Interprint, Durban

Contents

Foreword

In this, her second book on culinary culture, Renata Coetzee attempts the almost impossible task of recording the food habits and practices of the Black man of southern Africa. It is not easy to find the way to the Black man's soul; through her arduous research and sensitive understanding of a culture so unlike her own, Renata Coetzee has succeeded in opening a door, in offering her readers a personal glimpse into the Black home and hearth.

The Black man's conditions of life have been substantially changed by the advent of the White man in Africa; he has had to adapt himself to completely new circumstances, during which adaptation he lost much of his African way of life. This way of life included certain methods of producing foodstuffs, their preparation and the manner in which the food was eaten – in other words, the composition of the Black man's traditional diet was largely altered.

Renata Coetzee is spurred on by a scholarly urgency to 'observe and record the ways of pristine Africa' before, as she puts it, 'the unrestrained forces of change eradicate all the traditions and practices of the past . . .' Her approach is cross-cultured with an historical depth, and is both scholarly and disciplined.

In dealing with indigenous food habits and practices, the author clearly depicts the associated behaviour patterns which form part of the courtesy code of the Black man. She confirms the inseparability of cultural aspects about which we are so often told by anthropologists. She has been able to show the interrelatedness of food habits and practices, behaviour patterns associated therewith and the dictates of custom and tradition.

Apart from the scientific identification of food plants, the book is presented in simple, everyday English – a fact which will make it accessible and enjoyable to both the scholar and the man in the street.

I wish her every success in the publication of this book.

Vincent Z. Gitywa
Associate Professor
Department of African Studies
University of Fort Hare, CP
Republic of South Africa

Acknowledgements

I am deeply indebted to the Black people from various areas of southern Africa who assisted me in documenting traditional recipes before these disappear in the onslaught of 20th-century technology.

In the words of Enos Xotyeni of the East London Museum who contributed many of the Xhosa recipes:

> Many of these dishes are no more eaten by the sophisticated urban Africans. They frown upon them. Some are really disappearing. Many Africans have copied the Western or pro-Western dishes. The traditional way of roasting meat has been over-shadowed by frying: more especially the women are the easiest to be swayed towards new introductions. The other reason could be the easy and quick preparation or cooking of Western foods. (Some are readymade and thus make the labour short.) These people give no exercise to their bodies which results in too much obesity, high blood pressure, heart disease among who stay in towns. The country folk are still quite resistant to these diseases.

Although the present tense is used throughout, many of the Black African customs have disappeared or are fast disappearing. The recipes have been selected to give an overview of the food culture in the southern part of the African continent, but it remains for people who have grown up in a specific tradition and can draw from the recollections of their grandparents, to record the complete food culture of the various peoples.

Interesting anecdotes that highlight traditional food habits like folklore, riddles, proverbs, etc., are also included as these subtly add to the atmosphere of the past.

For discussion and demonstrations on Sotho food, my sincere thanks to Alina Mokati, Suzan Fihlo, Agnes Phakoe and Emily Monethi.

In Venda I received valuable assistance from Tryphina Chigovha, Pricilla Nthai and Joyce Raimaite.

Hulda Phalatse of the Hebron College of Education, Bophutatswana, reviewed Tswana recipes and student dietitians from Medunsa University assisted with their traditional recipes.

Xhosa recipes were supplied by Enos Xotyeni, Margaret Mthembu and Zutkiswe Zondeki.

The Zulu and Swazi food habits were explained by various people in these communities.

To all these friendly people who gave so generously of their time and wealth of tradition, my deepest and sincerest thanks.

For reading the manuscript for anthropological content, my appreciation to Professors Vincent Gitywa, Bill van Niekerk and Mesdames Margaret Shaw and Ansie Hof. Botanical names were scrutinised by

Barbara van Gass and Bantu words checked by Dr Rosalie Findlayson. Professor Ian Ferguson and Mesdames Petrovna Metelerkamp and Truida Prekel spent many hours editing the manuscript and Naomi van Reenen patiently retyped all new concepts. This company of friends made this work possible.

Because I had to attend to a career as well, my mother and aunt Miriam undertook the tedious routine jobs associated with the writing of a book. My sincere thanks to them.

I am deeply grateful to my friends for their encouragement to continue the research.

As a nutritionist, I sincerely hope that these recipes will facilitate the prescription of appropriate diets for Black patients, and that they will be incorporated in the syllabi of schools and colleges teaching food science and nutrition. To this end the traditional recipes for baby food and foods served to pregnant women were purposely omitted, since these practices could lead to malnutrition.

Renata Coetzee

PART 1

CULTURAL
ROOTS

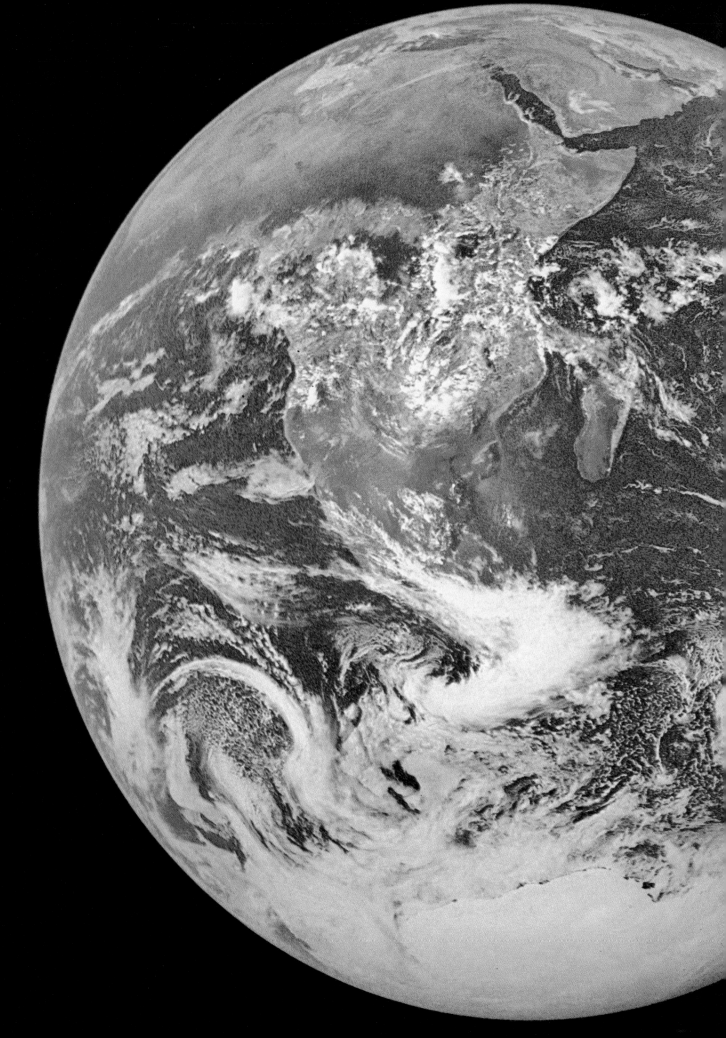

The planet Earth has six continents
rising from restless oceans.
Of these, Africa holds a prominent
position, separating the Indian and
Atlantic oceans and spreading its
land masses into both the northern
and southern hemispheres.

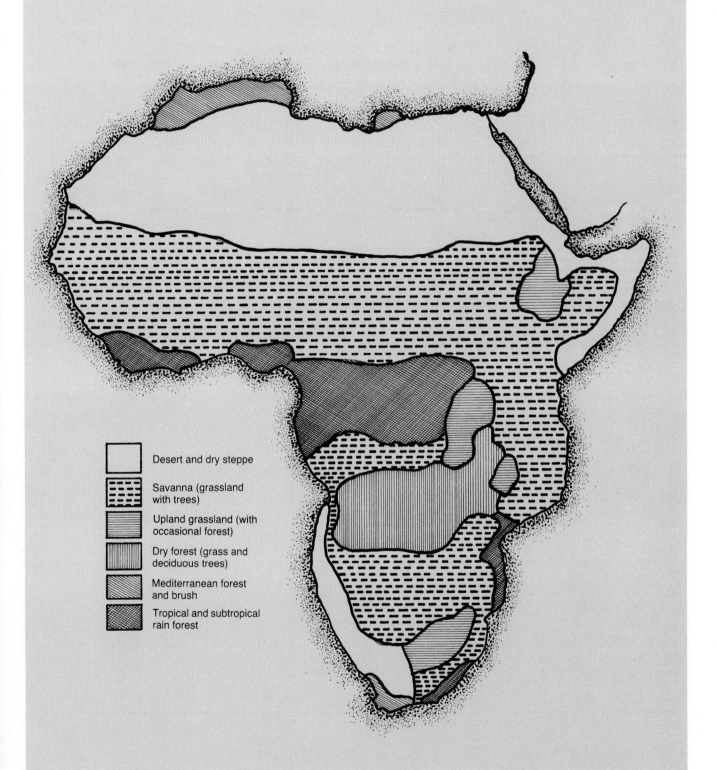

Legend

☐	Desert and dry steppe
▤	Savanna (grassland with trees)
▥	Upland grassland (with occasional forest)
▥	Dry forest (grass and deciduous trees)
▨	Mediterranean forest and brush
▨	Tropical and subtropical rain forest

Vegetation zones of Africa

AFRICA – the fascinating continent

Africa has a surface area of about 30 300 000 square kilometres, second only to Eurasia in size, but nearly 40% larger than the Soviet Union and three times that of the United States of America.

Geologically, Africa consists mainly of a single rigid rock of marine origin which, it is estimated, was deposited some 200 million years ago. Later this block rose up to thousands of metres above sea level. The result was the formation of large plateaus, some more than 2 000 metres high, infrequently interrupted by mountain ridges of lesser format than those on other continents.

These extensive plateaus gave rise to vegetation of savanna or grasslands with scattered trees, mainly baobabs or species of Acacia when rainfall is sufficient, and thorny scrubs in more arid regions. The so-called 'dry forest' of flat-topped deciduous trees covers large areas of the continent. This is the most prevalent vegetation in Africa. Tropical jungles or rain forests are sparsely spread, in contrast to popular belief.

The desert areas of Africa are expansive but belie the concept of barren sand dunes. Most of these areas support scattered shrubs, sometimes grass pastures and often shady oases.

This résumé briefly states the characteristics of Africa, part of the 'Third World' of modern history, as it stands with one foot in restful antiquity and the other in the dynamic 20th century.

Before the unrestrained forces of change eradicate all the traditions and practices of the past, it is imperative that we observe and record the ways of pristine Africa.

The origin of African man

While the African land masses were slowly rising out of the ocean bed, the same forces were causing giant fractures in the earth crust along a north–south line. These trenches of which several are lower than sea level, formed the Great Lakes on the face of Africa.

Along this enormous rift of the African continent, traces of the earliest man have been found. The excavations of the famed Drs Leakey, a husband-and-wife team, suggest that Africa could well be the cradle of man.

Although the very earliest ages of man are shrouded in obscurity, his later descendants have been identified by palaentologists, anthropologists and historians. One such a renowned palaentologist and anatomist, Professor Raymond Dart, made an extensive study of the skulls which were recovered throughout the African continent. The cranial characteristics of these skulls led him to the conclusion that three main racial groups once lived and wandered in ancient Africa.

The Negroid people, a black-skinned race, left traces of their origin along the Congo basin, whereas the brown-skinned Hamites, stemming from the east, lived towards the north of the African continent. Relics of a third group, the copper-skinned San people, can be traced virtually throughout the whole continent.

These three groups amalgamated and their descendants constitute the main populace of the 350 million inhabitants who live in 20th-century Africa. The descendants of the original groups can today be classified roughly into six major races, namely the Negroes, Nilotes, Semites, Hamites, African Negroids and Khoisan peoples. Contemporary African man can therefore trace his roots back into antiquity.

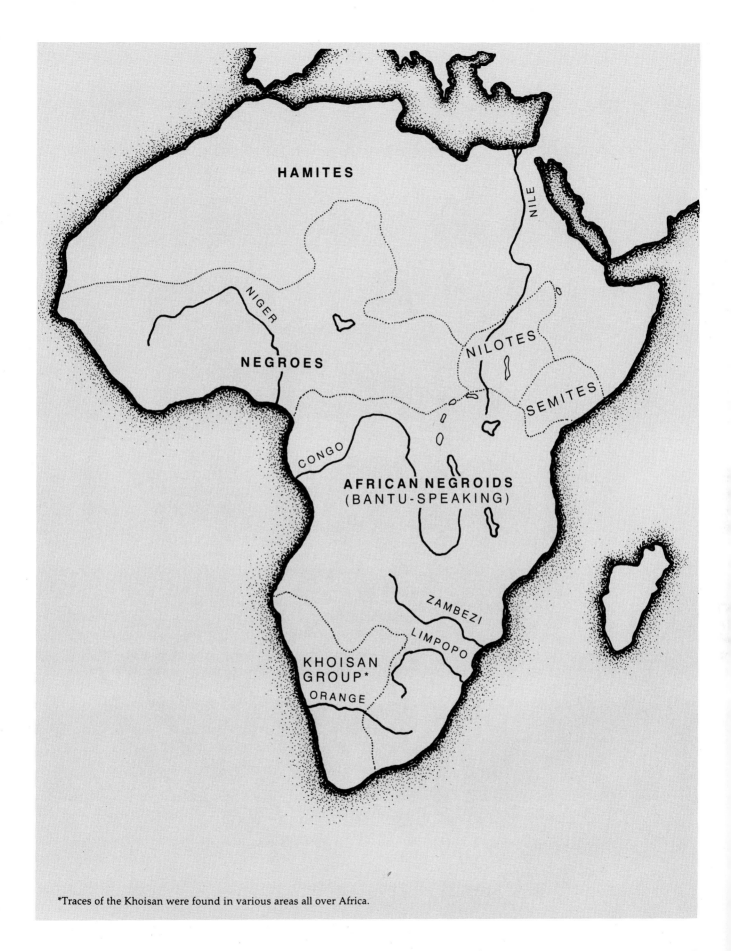

HAMITES

NILE

NIGER

NEGROES

NILOTES

SEMITES

CONGO

AFRICAN NEGROIDS
(BANTU-SPEAKING)

ZAMBEZI

LIMPOPO

**KHOISAN
GROUP***

ORANGE

*Traces of the Khoisan were found in various areas all over Africa.

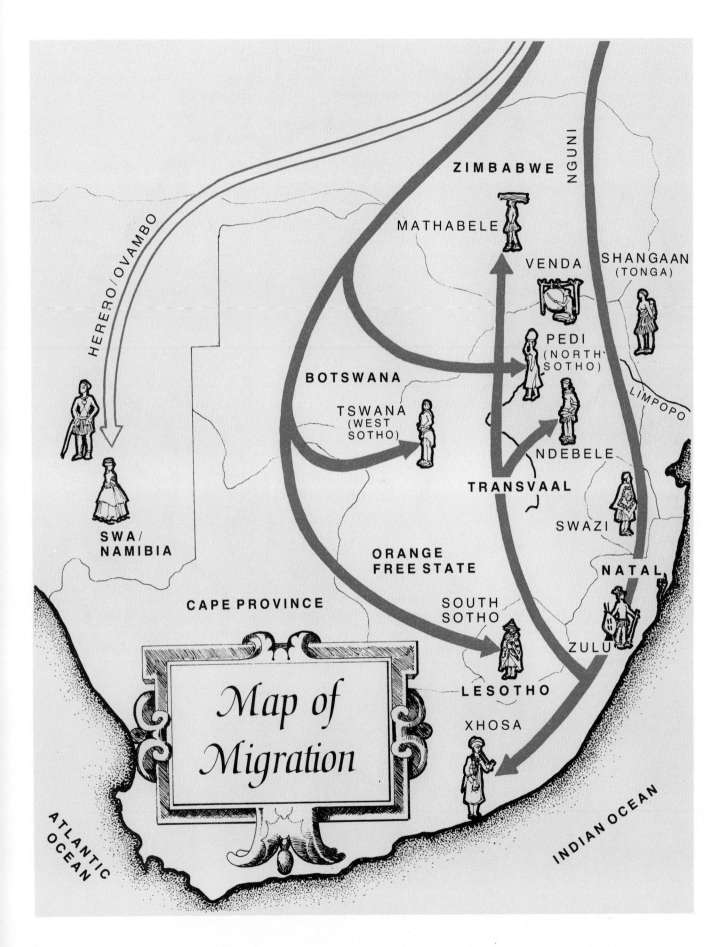

HERERO/OVAMBO

SWA/
NAMIBIA

ZIMBABWE

NGUNI

MATHABELE

VENDA

SHANGAAN
(TONGA)

PEDI
(NORTH
SOTHO)

BOTSWANA

TSWANA
(WEST
SOTHO)

LIMPOPO

NDEBELE

TRANSVAAL

SWAZI

ORANGE
FREE STATE

NATAL

CAPE PROVINCE

SOUTH
SOTHO

ZULU

Map of Migration

LESOTHO

XHOSA

ATLANTIC
OCEAN

INDIAN OCEAN

Roots of the southern African negroid peoples

The contact between the two original groups, the Negroes and the Hamites, resulted in a new race, the Negroid African. Initially they lived in the vicinity of the Great Lakes, but they slowly moved southwards and today occupy most of the landmass south of the Lakes.

The southward movement was unhurried and followed routes dictated by the needs of the expanding family clans of the African Negroid people, as well as by the geographical, climatic and political demands of the vast and often inhospitable continent.

Many theories, based on conjecture, are held on these movements of the early African people, but it is generally accepted that they gradually split into several streams, and over a period of approximately 2 000 years meandered into the most remote reaches of the subcontinent.

Four main groups eventually crossed the Limpopo River. The Nguni, Tsonga and Venda spread into the luxuriant eastern regions and the Sotho occupied the central part of the country.

The Nguni in turn gave rise to the Swazi, the Zulu, the Xhosa and the Ndebele peoples and the Sotho group to the North, South and West Sotho peoples.

The southward movement became more stabilised towards the end of the 18th century, by which time these peoples had settled down in organised groups, subdivided into smaller groups or units and had established distinctive cultural patterns.

These people are the ancestors of the peoples in South Africa today, which consist of the following:*

Main groups	Nations (peoples)	Main subgroups
Nguni	Swazi	Nkosi Dlamini
		Makhandzambili
	Zulu	Usutu
		Nyuswa
		Ngwane
		Mabaso
		Mkhize
		Buthelezi
		Qwabe
		Thembu
		Mthethwa
		Nxumalo
	Ndebele	Langa
		Moletlane
		Manala
		Ndzundza
	Xhosa	Ngqika
		Gcaleka
		Gqunukhwebe
		Thembu
		Bomvana
		Mpondo
		Mfengu
		Hlubi
		Bhaca
		Nhlangwini
Sotho	South Sotho	Kwena
		Kgatla
		Tlokoa
		Taung
		Tebele
		Vundle
	North Sotho	Pedi
		Koni
		Phalaborwa
		Lobedu
		Kutswe
	West Sotho	Tswana
		Ngwato
		Kwena
		Kgatla
		Rolong
		Tlhaping
		Tlharo
Venda and Lemba		
Tsonga	Tsonga	Nhlanganu
		Nkuna
		Tembe
	Shangana	Tulilamahashe
		Shangana
		Nkuna

*Classification according to the late Professor J. B. Bruwer

Traditional kinship – a rare possession

The traditional family is known as a clan and the 50-odd subgroups mentioned in the foregoing classification consist of these smaller family units. The Zulu name for a clan is *uzalo,* the Xhosa speak of *isiduko,* while the Venda call it *mutupo.* Members of a clan are related through the founder of the clan, a common ancestor, often dated 12 to 15 generations past. Although clan members may live in different areas, they retain an affinity towards one another and a kinship based on mutual interests.

The clan members are further united through age groups according to the human life cycle. Each family member has importance as one of a particular age group, and the whole community takes a true interest in his or her development from one phase of growth to the next.

Friendships are formed in the same age group and they last throughout life. Passing from one phase to the next is cause for celebration for the whole clan, like the gathering for initiation ceremonies, wedding festivals and even 'passing on to the forefathers', funeral rites and funeral meals.

Similarly, group activities such as harvest festivals or rain-making ceremonies are celebrated by all clan members and every individual has a legitimate right to participate.

The traditional practice of grouping children in age groups and attaching importance to the life cycle of the individual clearly nurtures psychological security and fosters human beings with identity and dignity, which are rare attributes in modern life. This age-grouping practice is called *intanga* by the Nguni and *thaka* or *mohato* by the Sotho peoples.

Cultural roots

Many definitions of 'culture' exist, and one acceptable definition would be: 'Culture is that complex whole which includes knowledge, belief, art, law, morals, custom and any other capabilities and habits acquired by man as a member of society.' Culture is not genetically inherited by man, it has to be acquired.

Prior to and during the many centuries of the southward movement, the culture of the Black man of southern Africa was established. He was an agriculturalist and cattle owner, gained the skill to work in metals like iron, copper and gold, and developed a social system that gave both security and dignity to the individual in the traditional society.

Early written testimony of the way of life of the people south of the Limpopo River is rare, but shipwrecked travellers left valuable records as early as 1552. Survivors of the São João, the São Bento, the Santo Thomé and the Saint Alberto, all stranded on the southeastern coast of Africa before the year 1600, recorded that they had met tribes that were tilling the soil, planting, and tending their herds. In the words of one of these journalists, 'these people are herdsmen and cultivators of the ground, by which means they subsist. They cultivate millet, which is white and the size of peppercorn; it is the fruit of a plant of the size and appearance of a reed. Of this millet, ground between two stones or in wooden mortars, they make flour, and of this they make cakes, which they cook among embers. Of the same grain they make wine, mixing it with a quantity of water which, when it has fermented in a vessel of clay and has cooled and turned sour, they drink with great enjoyment. Their cattle are very fat, tender, well flavoured and large, the pastures being very rich. They use milk and the butter which they make from it.' Describing the fermented liquor referred to as 'wine' above, a later traveller (from 1803 to 1806) Dr Lichtenstein, remarked: 'They also make from it [millet] a fermented liquor, which tastes almost like beer, but of a much more intoxicating quality, and much sooner spoiled: they call it *tjaloa*. A better sort is even made called *inguhja*, which is not unlike wine, and they make vinegar of it, which they call *tjala* ... These different liquors are obtained according to the different degrees of fermentation which the millet undergoes by being put for a certain time, mixed with water, into beer baskets, which have had fermented matter in them. In the place of sieves for straining it they use the nests which many sorts of African loxia build with the wooly parts of particular plants.'

From an old Africana drawing

Reference to birds' nests as beer sieves was also made by an early traveller, Captain Lodewyk Alberti, who described these nests as being cone-shaped and very tightly woven from small aloe leaves.

It is interesting to read what these early writers observed in respect of the mode of dress: 'The dress is a mantle of ox-hide, with the hair outwards, which they rub with grease to make it soft. They are shod with two or three soles of raw leather fastened together in a round shape and secured to the feet with straps, in these they can run with great lightness.' Other writers mentioned sandals made of elephant hide. There are also references to skins for clothing. 'They are clothed in skins which hang over their shoulders to the knees; these are cow-hides, but they have the art of dressing them till they are as soft as velvet.' Regarding accessories: 'They all carry sticks in the hands, with a tail at the end like the brush of a fox, which serves them as a handkerchief and fan.' This observation was confirmed by later journalists, and an additional function for this stick was mentioned – that of shading the eyes from the sun.

Early travellers also left us a record of the homesteads of the inhabitants: 'They live in small villages, in huts made of reed mats. They surround the huts with a hedge, within which they keep the cattle. They obey chiefs whom they call Intosis.' Other writers added that these people were also 'so hospitable that at every kraal there was a hut kept purposely for the accommodation of strangers. They are a social people, they never pass each other without stopping and conversing.'

These old documents clearly portray the established cultural patterns of the people who had journeyed from the Great Lakes. Their cultural practices were developed mainly during the centuries of movement over the face of Africa and the similarities in cultural customs of the different peoples in southern Africa confirm their common ancestry.

These cultural patterns were prevalent in traditional society until recently and in some remote villages they can still be observed untainted by technological intrusion. These rare places are invaluable for recording and preserving the cultural roots of the 20th century Black peoples and this study examines the traditional food practices and daily living patterns of traditional life.

The main cultural characteristics and practices pertaining to food habits and daily life are such that generalised descriptions of these can be attempted, and differences can be indicated where significant.

1 Venda courtyard

The Venda courtyard with all the equipment and ingredients necessary to prepare 'king's porridge': marula pounding block and maize ears; winnowing basket, basket in which to carry porridge, meal calabash and scoop, pottery side dish of dried ants, wooden plate with prepared porridge and the clay pot, wooden spoon and stirring stick used when cooking the porridge. In Sotho societies, the hearth or fireplace is usually in the courtyard and is only moved inside in bad weather. Sometimes a separate hut is used for the preparation of food.

◁ **2 Putu**

This mealie dish is a favourite in the Nguni society.

The hearth is inside the home, where food is traditionally served on communal eating mats. Meat, however, is dished into wooden bowls.

Putu is served with one of various side dishes such as pumpkin slices (top right); amadumbes (on the right: cooked and peeled in the front bowl and raw and unpeeled in the back bowl); and wild spinach *(imifino)* (front).

◁ **3** *Umcuku*

Umcuku, a Nguni favourite, is prepared by grinding dried mealies on the grindstone and catching it on the grain mat. The ground maize is stored in the small basket (on the grain mat) until the dish is completed by mixing it with curds *(amasi)*.

The fresh milk is poured from the wooden milk pails (in the background) into the *amasi* calabashes with wooden stoppers and whey is drawn off through a hole in the bottom of the calabash (visible on the inverted *amasi* calabash).

Curds and ground maize (in open calabashes) are then mixed to prepare the dish on the basketry plate.

Each family member has his own spoon to eat from the communal plate. After being washed, these spoons are replaced in the plaited-reed spoon bag.

◁ 4 Cultivated crops grown around a Venda village

Traditional crops, some indigenous, some originating in the Middle East and South America, have been cultivated in African societies for centuries. The innovative African women developed a variety of traditional dishes from these ingredients.

The artistic decoration on the Venda floor and the utensils match the eye-pleasing traditional crops – maize and sorghum ears, melons and pumpkins – the latter providing an array of possibilities. *From left to right:* Dried pumpkin flowers; dried pumpkin leaves; fresh pumpkin flowers and fresh pumpkin with dried pumpkin seeds next to it. The pumpkin flowers are a great delicacy and are made into a very special stew for the groom on the morning of the Venda wedding.

The village

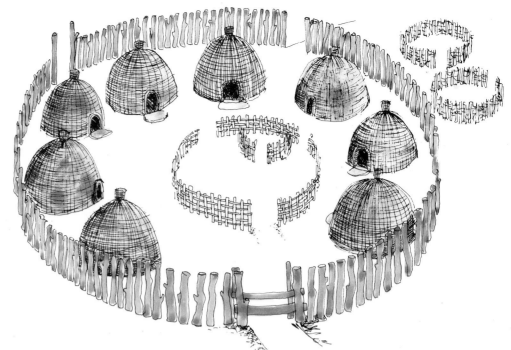

Cultural life is centred on the activities of the village. In the tranquil atmosphere of the village the young are versed in age-old traditions and practices and purposely moulded for their future role in society. In this manner the village nurtures the identity of its members and sustains the culture of the tribe. The cherished village is known as *motse* to the Sotho, *umzi* to the Xhosa and *umuzi* to the Zulu.

Villages vary in size according to the cultural customs of the different peoples. In some units the village comprises the homesteads of the different wives and children of the patriarch, whereas in other villages several families group their homes together. These families are usually related, most frequently through the male lineage. In other villages a whole clan live together in an extended community, but sub-units of related families continue to live in close proximity and retain their identity within their own group. Large villages of this kind sometimes boast as many as several thousand inhabitants.

The layout of the village has an interesting, well-organised pattern relating to the cultural practice of the people. Usually the homesteads are arranged either in full or in semi-circles around a central open space, with the doors of all the homes facing this central area. This space is enclosed by a fence of wooden poles, thorny shrubs, or a stacked stone wall, and serves as a cattle fold with an enclosure for small stock at one side.

At night this area offers shelter to the cattle, the most prized possession of the village. During the day it serves as the venue of all tribal ceremonies and other important appointments. As the focal point of the village, it is fraught with taboos. For example, women may only enter it on special occasions such as marriage festivals: it is here that a bride ceremoniously bids farewell to her family before she accompanies her husband to his village.

Near the cattle byre (or kraal), usually in the shade of a spreading tree, is the seat of the elders of the village. The headman and his councillors gather daily to discuss problems affecting the group as a whole and solutions are considered in accordance with traditional customs. Messengers and visitors to the village are also directed here to be interviewed or to convey their news. The court of justice regularly meets at this site to settle squabbles and to bring transgressors to trial. If they are found guilty, suitable punishment is decreed by the wise old councillors. This meeting place is held in high esteem by all African communities: all the Sotho villages have their *kgotla* or *kgoro* and the Zulu villages their *isibaya* or *ibandla*. In some Nguni tribes the meeting place of the men is between the kraal gate and the main hut; it is known as *inkundla*.

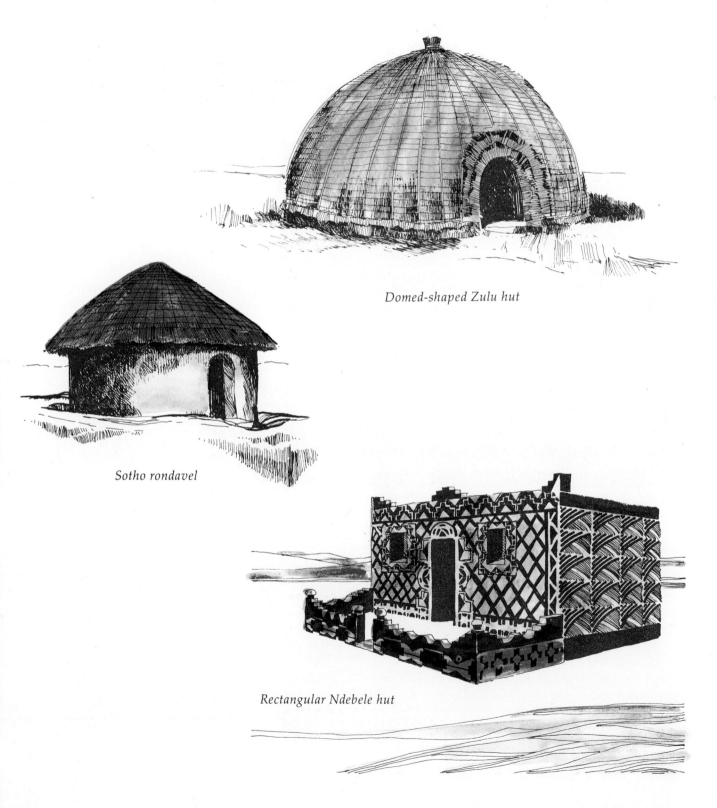

Domed-shaped Zulu hut

Sotho rondavel

Rectangular Ndebele hut

The homestead

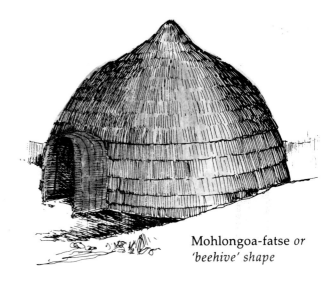

Mohlongoa-fatse *or* *'beehive' shape*

The architecture of the homesteads of the different cultural groups has a specific charm and beauty in the simplicity of line and the balance of form. For building material, African people look to nature and skilfully utilise what their surroundings offer: wooden poles, saplings, reeds, grass and clay.

Traditional African architecture shows a round floor plan, and two main types of constructions are found south of the Limpopo – the domed hut and the rondavel. The origin of these two designs has been studied by many anthropologists and the general conclusion is that the rondavel design was adopted from eastern Hamitic and Sudanic Negro cultures before the people set out on their southward migration.

The domed hut developed from the original *mohlongoa-fatse*, a 'beehive' structure, which consisted of saplings planted upright in a circle and tied together at the top to provide a cone-shaped roof. Many variations of domed hut constructions have been developed through the years.

In earlier times travellers described huts in the shape of swallows' nests, i.e. round, low constructions with elongated entrance passages. These older constructions gradually disappeared and a new rectangular design was introduced. The latter was developed after contact had been made with immigrants from Europe. The architecture of the Ndebele is noted for its rectangular houses, the elongated walls decorated in brightly coloured designs.

The Zulu and Swazi people use the dome-shaped design for their round homes, whereas the other African groups in southern Africa use mainly the rondavel construction, and to a lesser extent the rectangular design.

The round Zulu *indlu* is indeed a work of art. At the start of the construction a circular furrow, roughly 15 cm deep and 15 cm wide, with a diameter of 15 m, is made in the soil. A row of saplings is planted in this circle and a second row planted inside the circle leaning outwards at an angle of roughly 30 degrees. Where the two rows meet, the saplings are tied down securely with a strong, twined grass cord. The tops of the saplings are then bent down and fastened together to form a framework for the dome. The whole construction

Inside My Zulu Hut

It is a hive
without any bees
to build the walls
with golden bricks of honey.
A cave cluttered
with a millstone,
calabashes of sour milk
claypots of foaming beer
sleeping grass mats
wooden head rests
tanned goat skins
tied with *riempies*
to wattle rafters
blackened by the smoke
of kneaded cow dung
burning under
the three-legged pot
on the earthen floor
to cook my porridge.

Oswald Mbuyiseni Mtshali,
Sounds of a cowhide drum

25

is skilfully thatched with bundles of tall grass and overlaid with tightly woven grass mats. The inside of this construction is neatly finished off with plaited grass mats and the floor plastered with clay or a mixture of clay and cow dung. The doorway is usually closed off with plaited grass mats which can be rolled up and tied back.

The art of building is not confined to a few artisans and both the men and the women of the village participate in the work. The building procedure is as follows: The prospective home builder tells his wife to brew a quantity of beer, and he informs his neighbours of his intention to build a home and invites them over. On a specific day all his friends arrive and the whole building process becomes a community project. Interspersed with beer drinking, the men usually chop the saplings and construct the framework, while the art of covering the frame with thatching and mat work is the responsibility of the women. Everybody lends a hand, even passersby who are then also entitled to a swig from the beer pot. When the home is finally completed, the celebrations proper are merrily enjoyed by all the workers to mark a happy occasion.

The rondavel type of home of the Sotho people differs from the dome-shape construction in that a separate roof rests on the walls of the house. A cylindrical wall is constructed from saplings or saplings and additional material, for example grass or clay. On this wall rests the roof, which is conical in shape. The roof usually has a framework made from wooden poles, and this is skilfully covered with thatching grass or reeds. The layers of thatching form a protective covering and are tied down at regular intervals to secure the roof against wind and rain. The floors of these rondavels are raised platforms and the entrance is provided with several steps. The doorway is customarily closed off by a wooden door.

Among some groups such as the Venda and North and West Sotho, the different households in a village are separated by a screen constructed from reeds, walls or wooden fences. These private porches or yards are called *lapas* in some communities and are extensions of the homes. Their floors are usually plastered and both a front and a back porch are often constructed, the front to receive visitors while the back porch is used for food preparation. The pounding block, grinding stones and storage containers for dried grain and other foods, as well as the hearth for cooking when the weather is fine, are all on the back porch.

The *lapa* is therefore an integral part of the household and even in polygamous societies each wife is entitled to her own *lapa* and her own home. Here she receives her friends and family and toddlers play under the watchful eyes of their mothers while the latter fulfil their chores.

Construction of the framework of a grass ▷
Zulu hut. The frame is covered with grass
mats and grass thatch

The arch of the door is tied down firmly

A series of arches completes the doorway

Four series of lath arches are constructed to complete the framework

27

The home interior

PLAN OF A ZULU HUT

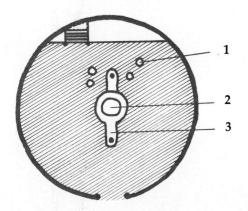

1 Indent in floor for round-bottomed pots

2 Hearth (iziko)

3 Raised wings (izimpundu)

The single-roomed house of the African village dweller has certain areas that the uninformed might desecrate. In the Zulu society, for instance, the right half of the hut as seen from the door, belongs to the wife, whereas the left half is the domain of the man.

The hearth is constructed in the centre of the hut. The *iziko* of the Zulu people is a raised platform with three supporting hearth stones for the cooking pot. The *choto* of the Shona, however, is a depression in the floor of about 9 cm deep and 40 cm across with three hearth stones to support the clay cooking pot. These two hearth constructions have been adopted by most South African groups.

Around the hearth, indents in the floor provide rests for the round clay pots. These are usually stored on a raised platform at the back of the hut and this storage platform is a sacred place, the dwelling place of the 'spirits of the forefathers'. This storage platform is called *umsamo* by the Zulus, *mahaolwana* by the South Sotho and *rukura* by the Shona. It is a shelf of solid clay built about half a metre above the ground and is roughly one metre long, 30 cm wide and is built by the woman of the house. Some women have become known as specialists in the art of building these sacred 'shrines'.

Occasionally a shelf is built above the platform for storing grain and eating vessels such as wooden bowls and spoons. Knives, assegais and sickles, however, are stuck into the thatch for safe keeping.

Directly above the hearth, against the roof, maize cobs are usually stored so that they may be preserved by the smoke of the hearth fire.

About one metre from the fireplace the father's special seat is placed where he warms himself at the fire. It is often made of a tree trunk and is reserved for the man of the house; not even a visitor or friend may sit on it. A clay ledge along the wall to the side of the door and partly facing the hearth, is usually built as a seat for visitors.

Besides the neatly rolled sleeping mats and wooden neck rests, a few additional low stools might complete the contents of the home. During the day sleeping mats are stacked away against the wall and the sparsely covered floor therefore becomes the focus of attention. It is an attractive feature, often glossed with fat or a mixture of blood and clay or cow dung. The blood mixture gives it the appearance of a dark red marble slab. Some tribes prefer decorations on the floor and make pleasing geometric designs in the wet clay that create a rippled effect when they dry. To obtain the shiny black floors preferred by some Zulu groups, charcoal is rubbed into the floor and covered with the black juice of the bulb of the *Hypoxis oligotricha* plant. The latter binds the charcoal and imparts a high gloss to the floor.

Sometimes there are separate huts which serve as dwellings, kitchens, storage huts and huts for visitors. These are very sparsely furnished, only containing mats or, in the case of the Tswana, animal skins and essential utensils.

The uncluttered arrangement of the interiors displays handcrafted utensils like the beautifully moulded clay pots, artistically carved wooden bowls, decorated calabashes and plaited and twined baskets and mats in a pleasing composition of unpretentious, attractive design.

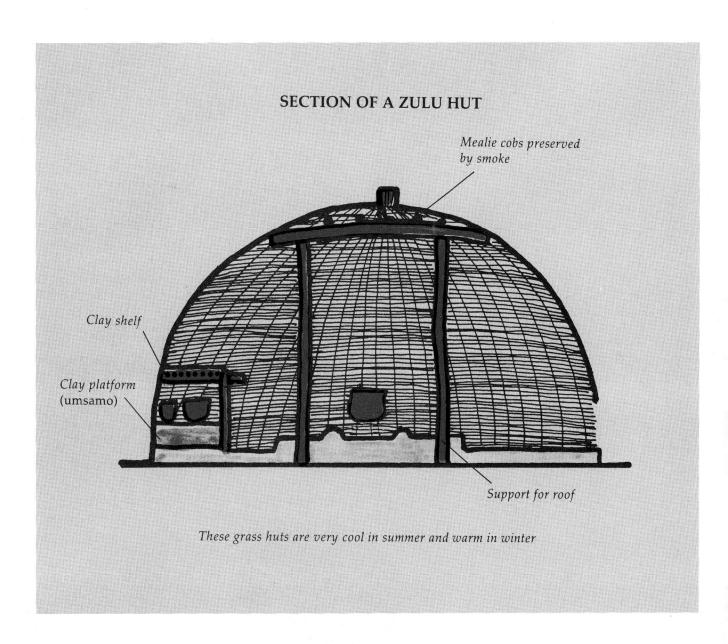

SECTION OF A ZULU HUT

Mealie cobs preserved by smoke

Clay shelf

Clay platform (umsamo)

Support for roof

These grass huts are very cool in summer and warm in winter

Household utensils

Household utensils are handcrafted. Some individuals become known as specialist potters, woodcarvers, basket makers and calabash decorators, and their creations are much sought after by their fellow tribesmen for both their functional and aesthetic qualities. These articles usually change hands through bartering – for the amount of grain they hold, for livestock when large containers for granaries are at stake, or for a service rendered, like the weeding of a field.

Women are the potters and calabash decorators and men are responsible for making wooden utensils. Basketry is practised by both sexes. Many different designs and variations of the four basic crafts are found in southern Africa, varying according to tradition and the personal style of the particular artist.

Pottery utensils

The clay pots of a household are made or acquired for a specific purpose, depending on the eating habits and customs of the group. The designations of pots are indicated by their characteristic shape and decoration.

The pots common to most households are water pots, i.e. pots used for carrying water on the head from the water source to the home and for storage in the home. The water in these porous earthernware pots remains cool and refreshing owing to the continuous evaporation of water from the outer surface.

Pots made for cooking differ from water pots in having larger openings to facilitate the stirring of food. Various sizes of cooking pots are used in each household: a large pot for the cereal or cereal-and-bean main dish, and smaller pots for side dishes like leafy green vegetables, pumpkin or meat. Shallow dishes are versatile and serve as lids for cooking pots, as 'frying pans' for delicacies like pumpkin pips, flying ants or locusts and as utensils for serving food or as plates. The size of these shallow dishes varies according to use, for instance individual eating dishes are smaller than communal eating dishes. The 'frying pan' is often a potsherd or a specially made utensil that resembles a potsherd.

31

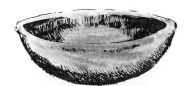

Handwash basin

Cooking pot

Water or beverage pot

*Smoothing the inside surface of
a beer container being made
by the coil method*

Small, round clay pots serve as drinking vessels. Those for fermented beverages usually have smaller openings than those for water, the only two beverages served in the traditional diet of the Black people.

Beer made from fermented cereal plays an important part in social life as well as in rituals and ceremonies. Consequently, the beer pots are the most ornately decorated pots in the household. Special drinking vessels are made for 'honoured guests' and are used for entertaining; these can therefore be considered 'party ware'. Designs of these party dishes are more often changed than are those of other pottery articles.

Extremely large pots are constructed for brewing beer and among some tribes these large containers are sunk partially into the ground, presumably to facilitate stirring and sieving and also to keep the beer cool.

Food storage pots are also large, and may be found inside the house or outside in the courtyard or *lapa*. Some big clay pots are protected by a roof or walls and serve as granaries.

Wash basins may be made of clay and a special basin-shaped container is traditionally used for hand washing before meals.

Other uses for clay vessels usually concern tribal rituals or social customs. In some groups, for instance, unmarried girls over the age of puberty are periodically examined by an old woman of the village to establish whether they are still virgins. The examinations are carried out near a water source, and each girl's mother gives her a pot to take with her. If she is still a virgin, she is allowed to fill it with water and take it to her father. If she has been seduced she may fill it only halfway, and the father then enquires about her lover and starts proceedings against him.

In areas where suitable clay for pottery is not readily available, calabashes and baskets are ingeniously substituted for the clay vessels, although the lack of a clay supply need not be the only reason for using calabashes or baskets.

Pottery techniques

Pottery techniques were closely guarded family secrets in earlier years, but gradually the custom of confining the art to members of particular families changed until all who were interested could try their hand. Nevertheless good pottery remains a specialised craft, usually practised by women.

Many taboos govern the making of clay pots. According to Professor V. Z. Gitywa, a dedicated researcher of the past and present arts and crafts of his people in Ciskei, many people believe that firing cracks the clay when handled by persons 'unsuited' to do so. Such people are women in their menses, someone who has been in contact with a corpse without ritual cleansing thereafter, or anybody who 'was not born to work with clay'. The lastmentioned belief cleverly excludes untalented people and ensures good pottery.

The potters are very meticulous about the symmetry and proportions of their creations and if vessels are misshapen when taken out of the kiln they are immediately destroyed.

Four basic moulding techniques have been recorded in southern Africa. The oldest technique is known as 'moulding from the lump'. A lump of prepared clay is placed on a base and the sides squeezed and smoothed to give the required size and shape. The 'coiling technique' is better known, where the body of the vessel is formed on the base with rolls of clay made between the palms of the hands and built up in a spiral fashion. The inside and outside of the vessel are finally smoothed with tools like shells, pebbles, corn husks or a piece of damp leather. The 'ring technique' is almost the same as coiling, except that the rings are obtained by making a large hole in a flat, round piece of clay. The base of the vessel is formed by bending the lower walls together after the body has been shaped. 'Building with lumps' describes the fourth process very well. Lumps of clay of no particular size are merely broken off the prepared material and the pieces are put together to form the lower half of the vessel wall. The lumps are smoothed out, the vessel is dried and the rest of the vessel completed by the addition of another 'wall' of clay lumps, with a repetition of the same procedure.

The clay is usually obtained in the vicinity of a river or a stream, from an antheap or any place where suitable clay can be found. Dry soil is usually ground on a flat stone to remove pebbles and vegetable impurities. Fillers in the form of ground potsherds or asbestos soils are sometimes added before the soil is mixed with water. The wet clay is kneaded on a flat stone to a plastic consistency and thus prepared, kept damp until moulding is completed. The vessels are then dried, while care is taken to prevent wind from hastening the drying process and inducing cracks in the clay.

After a few days of drying the vessels are fired. The kiln is usually a trench in the ground or a protective stone wall enclosure. Any person may prepare the kiln but the potter herself does the baking on a clear, windless day. Good weather is important to ensure even heat dispersion through the kiln. The pots are arranged in the kiln and filled and surrounded with dry grass, firewood or dry cow dung. The whole pile is set alight and after a few hours the products are inspected. A reddish-brown colour and a metallic sound when tapped indicate completion of the process.

The Zulu and Swazi usually prefer their pottery in black. This effect is obtained by smoking the fire pots in grass fires.

The decorations on the vessels vary according to tradition or designs favoured by the potter. Geometric patterns are often used in southern Africa. Designs are made in soft clay on the outer wall of the pot with a pointed stick, thorn, shell or other tool. Relief decorations are traditionally made by the Zulu people by moulding clay pellets on to the outer surface of the vessel.

Colour is used as decoration in some areas. The Venda people use graphite for their shiny black design, others use ochre for brick-red colour, and white decorations are made with chalk.

Clay vessels used for serving and storing food and beverages, and for washing, are usually decorated whereas larger beer or brewing pots and cooking vessels are mostly left plain.

Several methods are employed to seal the completed pots which will be used to contain liquids, like cooling thin porridge in the vessel to leave a thin layer against the side. This layer is left to dry before it is peeled off. Other methods constitute smearing the pot with acacia gum, or cooking fat meat in the pot.

Pot ready for firing in the kiln

Zulu pot with pellet decorations

Venda dish

Calabash containers

Calabash containers are made from the hard-shelled fruit of gourds, a trailing plant which belongs to the family *Cucurbitaceae*. These plants are indigenous to the tropical areas of Africa but early travellers in the southern part of the continent recorded that 'gourds of many kinds' were also cultivated.

The preparation of calabash containers is not as specialised a craft as pottery, and has no taboos attached to it. Women make the calabash vessels by picking them when they are ripe and either dry or cook them to strengthen the skin and soften the outside. An opening of the desired size is cut in the gourd, the inside scooped out and it is further cleaned by swirling pepples, sand and water or even mealie seeds around inside it.

The utensils made from gourds depend upon the shape of the fruit, which grow into globular, pear, long-necked, double-bowl ('waisted'), and elongated shapes.

The pear and golublar shapes make excellent flasks or bowls for water or beer. They are also used as containers for milk as are the 'waisted' vessels. Sour milk, relished by all African people, is fermented preferably in calabashes. A small hole is made in the bottom of the milk calabash to draw off the whey and the mouth of the flask is closed with a mealie-cob stopper. A little sour milk is usually left in the calabash to start the next fermentation process.

The sour milk calabash is called *ingula* by the Tsonga: the name is onomatopoeic and imitates the sound made by the fermenting milk. A vivid description of the use of milk flasks in the Xhosa community has been given by a research worker, Dr Fox, who is a pioneer researcher on the composition of South African foods: 'The warm milk is poured straight from the milking into a calabash already containing a little *amasi* (sour milk). A common sight at midday at the kraals, whilst milking is proceeding, is an array of calabashes waiting in the sun to be filled. If whey separates, it is drunk as *intloya* especially in hot weather to quench thirst whilst the hard curd is termed *ingqaka*. If the product is too sour it is mixed with fresh milk.'

Milk calabashes have a particular place in the home, sometimes opposite the door but more often on the man's side of the hut. There are, however, special small calabashes used for children and these frequently hang on the mother's side of the hut so that she has easy access to them. For a journey the child's calabash is encased in a net of twined grass to make it easier for the mother to carry. Milk taboos prevail in most tribes and people who are considered impure are often prohibited from touching milk calabashes. In some tribes all the milk calabashes, except those used by the children, are thrown out when a death occurs in the house.

In the Zulu household, beer and water calabashes are larger than those used for milk. These calabashes often have lids made from a piece of calabash cut away to form the opening or, alternatively, small basket caps serve as covers. A grass net often encloses these calabashes to facilitate transportation.

Small beaker-shaped calabashes are used as individual or communal drinking vessels among the Ndebele and in other societies. Dishes are made by cutting elongated gourds in half. These containers are also used as handwashing basins.

Long-necked gourds are used for ladles or scoops for both liquid and solid foods, the long neck being used as a handle. These vessels with handles are sometimes also used as drinking vessels or eating plates. Small herd boys frequently use this type of 'plate' but when it is used as a plate by a grown-up, it indicates that he is in a great hurry.

Calabashes are favourite storage containers for ingredients like freshly ground grain for porridge. In most households a small calabash is traditionally selected for use as a salt container.

Calabash decorations

Geometric designs are often seen on Venda and some Sotho calabashes. These designs are branded into the woodlike gourd skin with a hot iron, piece of wire or knife blade. These geometric patterns often depict tribal situations, for example where a village entrance is depicted as being protected against villains by a scorpion, geometric markings symbolise the entrance, the scorpion and the villains.

Strings of brightly coloured beads cover the calabashes of the Ndebele and some other groups, while the Nguni use brass or copper wire decorations on their calabashes. Both these techniques are obviously more recent, dating from the time when these decorating commodities became available.

Colour is also used as decoration and the warm yellow colour of the calabash is sometimes changed to white by scraping the cuticle to reveal the inner layer. A beautiful deep old rose colour is obtained by staining the calabashes with millet water.

Decorations are used on all calabashes, except milk calabashes. Butter is often made by churning cream in a calabash. This is not used as a food, but as a cosmetic to grease the skin. Small decorated calabashes are used for storing this cosmetic, and a young girl would present such a calabash containing grease to her 'favourite' amongst the young boys. Among the Xhosa this small calabash with its contents is called *ihlala*.

Basketry

Baskets are popular household utensils. Being light in weight they are preferred for the transport of food or other commodities in the traditional way – on top of the head. Because baskets are more easily transported and do not break as easily as earthenware or calabashes, tightly woven baskets, impervious to liquid, are preferred by the Zulus for the fermentation of beer.

Basketry articles found in most households are sleeping mats, grain mats, winnowing and carrying baskets, and beer strainers.

Each person has his or her own sleeping mat, but sometimes women have two, one of which is specifically used during menstruation. Small, tightly woven mats called *isithebe* by the Xhosa, are used by most tribes next to the grinding stone to collect the meal.

The winnowing basket is either a round, shallow tray or a basket with wide sloping sides. The dehusked grain is tossed to and fro and up and down in the basket so that the chaff is blown away by the wind, or it is poured off the basket onto a grass mat with a shaking movement to separate the chaff.

The carrying basket usually has a concave bottom to fit easily over

Decorated Venda milk calabash

and meal calabash

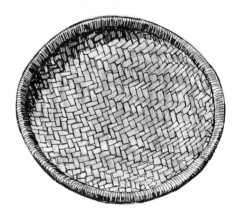

Venda winnowing basket

Sotho carrying basket

the head and the sloping sides accommodate a maximum load. Women carry goods in this way and the missionary-anthropologist Junod states: 'They are very clever at balancing it on their heads; it is very rarely that a woman old or young, lets her carrying basket fall. When empty it is turned upside down and serves as a hat. It is a really pretty sight to see the young girls starting out for the fields with their conical baskets standing straight up on their heads when they are travelling and when they arrive at a friendly village, they hold themselves perfectly upright, shooting glances here and there without stooping or turning their heads, till their friends rush out to meet them, seize their baskets and place them on the ground, in small holes which they hastily make in the sand. This is the first duty of hospitality amongst women!'

Beer strainers are elongated sacks with minute openings between the tightly woven strands. Fermented beer is forced through the stainer to clear it from impurities and mix it thoroughly. It is the custom among the Ndebele for a young, betrothed girl to send a beer strainer and a small grass broom to her future father-in-law, indicating that she would expect good beer and a clean homestead when she arrives at her future home!

Basketry is also used for food-serving utensils. The Nguni and some Sotho groups usually serve porridge on small closely woven mats, and in some areas meat is served on wicker trays. A special custom among the Venda and Lobedu calls for beautifully lidded baskets with an indented bottom for serving food to the head of the house. The food is dished onto a wooden plate, put into the bottom of the basket and presented to the lord and master with the lid on.

Baskets with lids are also used for storing valuables like the best grain, reserved for seed for the next planting season. Storage baskets can be of different shapes and sizes and very large ones sometimes serve as granaries. Some granary baskets are covered with clay and protected by a conical grass roof. Others are mounted on platforms either made of soil and covered with matting, or made of wood and mounted on stilts. Underground granaries were formally used to protect grain from marauding impi's and these baskets were then buried in pits.

Veld foods are collected to supplement the grain, and carrying baskets or specially constructed flexible bags are used for this purpose.

Bags are also constructed for travelling. These bags are tightly woven, have a sling to facilitate carrying and are covered by a sliding lid. Such travelling bags are used mainly by men. The Bantwane manufacture a special bag carried by young girls. This bag has an attractive open pattern created by sewing small rings together, resulting in a decorative article very suitable for young women.

These household utensils handcrafted from clay, wood, grass of gourds, reflect the warmth of the natural materials and are characterised by their individuality of design. Their functional application enhances their value as material culture treasures.

The array of basketry found in a home varies according to custom and availability of material for basket construction.

Zulu beer sieve

Swazi storage basket

36

Basketry techniques

Basketry is a specialised craft, although most women practise it to provide for their own household needs. Male basket workers tend to be very skilful, but no young man is ever forced to take up the profession unless his heart is in it. It remains a matter of individual genius and therefore never becomes a mechanical output as in the factories of the modern world.

There are two major techniques of basketry in southern Africa – weaving and sewing. Margaret Shaw, doyenne of research of these tangible cultural objects, distinguishes between the two techniques: 'In woven work two sets of elements are interlaced by crossing over and under each other to make a fabric. In sewn work one set of elements is sewn together by the other.'

Tools used in the production of basketry are those for cutting, like knives or spear blades, awls made from wood, bone, thorns or aloe leaves, and needles made from natural materials like a bone or a stick.

A great variety of materials is used for basketry. These are collected from nature and skilfully prepared for the particular basketry process. Grass stems are selected for delicate work and whole grasses are used for the base foundation in coiled sewn work. Sedge stems provide the most popular material. They may be used whole in woven articles or may be split, the pith removed and applied straight or twisted for the foundation or sewing element of sewn basketry. Sedges are used in beer strainers, food mats, grain bins, sleeping mats, roofs and other articles. Rushes with their thick rough texture are preferred for sleeping mats. In the northern part of South Africa the flexible stems of creepers are used to make baskets. For the base of the basket the trimmed stems are coiled and sewn together with thin strands of split stem.

Leaves from *Iridaceae, Strelizia,* 'baboon tails' and palm leaves are used for basketry. Especially the ilala palm leaves are picked in the coastal areas where they grow. These leaves are suitable for fine work as in beer strainers or tightly coiled baskets.

Colour decorations are introduced in basketry by weaving or sewing coloured strands into the design. All colour is obtained from local materials and sometimes plant strips are soaked in marshes, and dried in the sun to produce a reddish-brown colour, which is often deepened by a second treatment. Plant dyes are also used, usually by steeping the plant in boiling water to extract the colour and then adding the basketry material to be coloured.

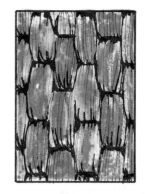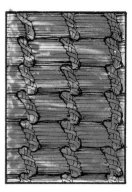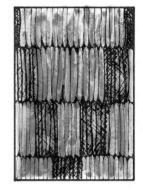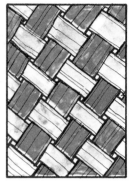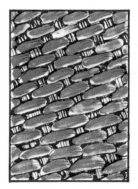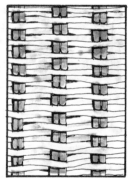

Basketry techniques

Wooden vessels

In southern Africa woodcarving has not reached as high a standard as basketry, probably owing to the relative scarcity of wood in many regions. In the rest of Africa this art is more developed, although utensils for food reached a fair standard among the Zulu, some Sotho groups and the Venda.

Several kinds of spoons are carved from wood: large spoons to serve food, ladles for serving beer and smaller spoons to eat with when the hands are considered impure. A special wooden spatula is made for stirring porridge after the flour has been beaten into the

Tsonga alliance spoon carved from a single piece of wood

Zulu meat bowl showing decorations on bottom

UTENSILS CARVED OUT OF WOOD

◁ **5 Grain storage and grain processing in the Xhosa community**

After reaping grain, it is stored in a well-constructed grass grainery. Numerous handcrafted utensils are used for processing the grain: conical-shaped carrying baskets, shallow, round winnowing baskets, wide-bottomed storage baskets with lids, a pounding block, grinding stones and eating mats to catch the grinds from the stone.

◁ **6 Household utensils**

Handcrafted household utensils,
similar to those used in a modern,
westernised kitchen.

Stirrer	('egg beater' of the traditional kitchen)
Whisk	(similar to a modern French whisk)
Sieve	(same use as in modern kitchen)
Skimmer	(same use as in modern kitchen)

◁ **8 Venda village with traditional
design on courtyard walls**

water by means of a wooden whisk, i.e. a stick with two wooden spikes in the point.

Meat dishes carved from wood are often very well designed and are attractive in their symmetry and proportions. The size of the bowl depends on the number of diners; very large containers are sometimes made for traditional festivals. Individual platters for serving food are also carved and are often flat with a slight rim.

The pounding block or mortar is made of wood. Long-stemmed pestles are used skilfully by the womenfolk, who usually work in pairs. They often alternate their strokes to break up the cereal seeds to the size desired for different dishes. Some pounding blocks are fitted with a stone in the bottom to reduce wear and tear on the wood.

Milk pails are carved from wood, the design depending on tribal milking customs, for example, some have handles, and some are on pedestals or have legs.

Woodcarving techniques

Traditionally no joinery is found in wooden articles, the whole piece being made from a solid piece of wood. The most amazing example of this technique can be seen in the Tsonga culture where two spoons are connected by a chain at least two metres long. The whole piece, including several links about 10 cm in length, is carved from a single piece of solid wood. The artist cannot afford to make a mistake – one slip of the knife would break the chain. These spoons are known to be used by people who wish to form an alliance, when they hang the chain over their shoulders while they eat from the same plate.

Trees are felled to obtain wood for the manufacture of these utensils. To aid in the cutting of large trees, a fire is made around the trunk. The cut wood is allowed to season and is continuously rubbed with fat during the preparation of the utensil to keep it from splitting.

Decorations on wooden utensils are of two kinds: carved or branded. Carved decorations mostly appear as grooves or ridges in a series of patterns. Branding is done with a hot iron, either in geometrical designs or to blacken the whole surface. Sometimes both techniques are used on the same article, creating an unusual effect. After preparation these utensils are greased and polished to a smooth, hard surface.

Zulu wooden spoons

QHUDE (The cock)

Wake up, daughter-in-law,
It is morning, oh, Mother!
There are sounds at the rocks,* oh, Mother!
Proclaiming the day, the water, O Cock!
There are sounds at the rocks, oh, Mother!
Proclaiming the day, there is no water!
Awake, there is no water!
Awake, daughter-in-law, there is no water!
Awake, daughter-in-law, there is no water!
Awake, daughter-in-law, there is no water!
They proclaim at the rocks!
It is morning, oh, the Cocks!
They proclaim at the rocks, oh, Mother!
It is morning, there is no water,
There is no water, there is no water, there is no water.

*In Xhosa folklore, 'rocks' usually refer to rocks found in or near a river.

Source: *The world of African song*, by Miriam Makeba.

A day at the traditional village

The people are astir early. In their own phrase, 'when the horns of the cattle are just visible', it is the sign to begin a new day. In traditional society, the sun rules time and just before it shows above the horizon, people roll out of their bedding.

The women usually get up first and wash before going about their morning work. They kindle a fire and the youths who have to take the cattle out to the pastures gather around for food. After milking the cows, these boys head for the best grazing site where the day is spent tending the cattle and goats.

In the meantime the men have dressed. They usually sleep a while longer than the rest of the family, especially since they often have to get up during the night to ensure that the cattle are safe in the cattle fold. The women see to it that there is water for the men to wash.

Full bathing is done later during the day at the bathing places in a river or at a water source. Bathing naked, like sleeping naked (rolled in blankets or a kaross), is customary, although the sexes usually bathe separately.

Soon after rising, the older men repair to the council-place where they spend the rest of the day, unless more important activities arise. The younger men have tasks to fulfil, like repairing huts or constructing granaries; and the older men go around to inspect this work or give instructions as to additional tasks to be performed.

The activities of the women revolve mainly around food, not only preparing meals but also producing food for the meals.

Towards mid-morning when the house has been swept and tidied, the first of the two daily meals is served. Various tasks have to be fulfilled to prepare the simple meal of either stiff porridge eaten as is, or soft porridge served with milk. Grain is fetched from the granaries and ground on the grinding stone to a fine meal for porridge or pounded in the wooden mortar to break the cereal seeds used for various dishes.

Water is hauled from the water source, and in some communities it is believed that a small pebble dropped in the pot will prevent the carrier from tripping while gracefully balancing the pot on the head, thus avoiding the misfortune of breaking the pot. Breaking a clay pot is considered a bad omen by some peoples.

The River

It whispers intimately
into clean-shaven pebbles
messages lost to boulders
crest-fallen trees standing by

Over and beyond the strains
of trees and boulders
howls the wind

Within the fingers of sulky dongas
crumbling with each stroke of thunder
within the humming silence of age
runs the river in between

Women come and go
they go and they come
water-buckets poised doeks
the sun's flint fingering as they walk
watched by brooding trees
clutching perilously at the ears
of the river in between

At the ears of the river
hugging the tortured course
are squeals of a donkey
and the pealing churchbell
angry with the mean sun
to quench man's parched voice
for neither here nor there
are voices heard crystal-clear

The clouds that gather
they go and they come
they come and they go
leaving the river without water

Sydney Sipho Sepamla
Hurry up to it!

Venda riddles

What is a drunken old man staggering?
A chameleon.

*What is like two squirrels fighting for
a hole in a tree trunk?*
Two women stamping grain.

*The tumba bird lays small eggs,
but grows very fat.*
A baobab tree, which grows
from small seeds.

What is a lover wearing five coats?
A mealie cob (a man in
love wears his best clothes
for his sweetheart to admire,
sometimes all at once).

What is a soft stick in a grove of trees?
A snake.

Firewood is collected; a large bundle of twigs cleverly tied together with grasses is transported on the head and dropped at the hut door with the traditional exclamation: 'Hu!'

When the porridge for the morning meal is cooked, it is ladled out into individual or communal containers to cool – wooden bowls, clay vessels, calabashes or eating mats, according to traditional practice. The food containers of the men, whether they be at the council-place or engaged in a task, are taken to them by the younger women. Water for washing hands before the meal and for drinking or rinsing the mouth afterwards, is also taken along. The women and children eat their share at the hut in the courtyard under the eaves if the weather permits, otherwise inside the home. Afterwards the bowls are fetched by the younger women and washed.

Depending on the season, most of the women would then set out to the fields or gardens, usually carrying their babies tied to their backs in soft goatskin wraps. Women are the agriculturalists in traditional society and cultivate most of the food. Work like sowing, hoeing, weeding or reaping is usually performed as a communal project although each wife cultivates a specific plot of land.

A few of the older women stay at home to take care of the children and the homesteads. They often contribute to the cooking pots by collecting veld food like wild spinach (*morogo/imifino*) for the evening meal, assisted by the older children carrying baskets. Some women stay at home to do pottery or basketry, but these occupations are usually practised between seasons when work in the fields is not as pressing.

In warmer areas, women might change their daily pattern. They tend their fields early in the morning before the first meal is served. During the heat of the day they spend their time at home with basket making or another occupation, only returning to the gardens or fields when it is cooler.

The men in the council-place while their time away by exchanging news, discussing affairs, settling disputes and announcing and receiving visitors. The men sit around in a haphazard way on stools or logs, against trees, or even lie about when nothing of importance is going on. Some may be engaged in handwork, like carving objects out of wood or horn, softening skins or weaving baskets. This informality, however, changes when their attention is demanded or when something important occurs. Then everybody sits up politely, listens attentively and participates actively in all proceedings.

The younger men do their chores in a happy atmosphere, joking and laughing while performing their tasks, and flirting with any young women who may pass their way.

'The late afternoon ushers in the less strenuous part of the day,' according to G. P. Lestrade, and he very aptly describes this time of day in the Northern Sotho society: 'Important matters at the council-place are settled by then, and it may be that someone, perhaps the head of the village, provides some beer for the men to drink. Beer-drinking is carried on with a fair amount of ceremonial. The pot is brought by a young woman who places it before the men. Several calabashes are brought at the same time. One of the men, usually the right-hand man of the village-head, takes charge, ladling out the beer with one calabash and pouring it into the others, which are handed round in turn. The man whose wife has provided the beer usually drinks first, to show that it is not poisoned. Others drink after him, the few calabashes being used by all the men in turn. Older and more important men are given the first share, others wait until later. If there is nothing to do at the council-place, the men will wander off, some going to visit friends, exchanging gossip and snuff, and possibly getting a calabash of beer in the process; or they may go off to a regular beer-party somewhere in the neighbourhood where some festive occasion is being celebrated. As the afternoon wears on and the men are more and more full of beer, voices grow higher and tempers may rise, vociferous disputes and wranglings and sometimes actual fighting may occur.

'The women also, on their return from the fields, or after their day's work at home, indulge in a certain amount of relaxation until the time comes for preparing the evening meal. They go out visiting, exchanging gossip, and in the case of older women, getting some snuff, and, if it is a fairly plentiful season, usually managing to obtain some beer as well. Women do not sit in on men's beer parties, but have some beer provided for them separately, which is drunk with considerably less ceremonial. In the course of such visits business transactions, such as the purchase and sale or exchange of household utensils or of foodstuffs, may take place. A good deal of good- or even ill-natured wrangling takes place over such deals.

'As the afternoon wears on towards dusk, the youths and boys come home with the stock which has been fed and watered. By this time the men will be drifting home gradually, and, as soon as the stock has returned, they will go to inspect it, after which the evening milking takes place.'

The evening meal is served when everybody has returned home. It is a family affair and is usually eaten outside, and inside the home when the weather is bad. The meal consists of two dishes: a main dish of cereal or a mixture of cereals or cereal combined with beans or other foods, while the side dish comprises either meat or wild leafy vegetables, or one of various other traditional dishes. This is the substantial meal of the day and most people eat quite a large amount.

After the evening meal, the family relaxes around their fires. This is the time for story telling. Older men may recount the heroic tales of battles long gone by, but especially the women are renowned for their stories. The relating of folklore is a most refined amusement. Children burst into laughter when the clever plans of Hare are described, shudder at the threatenings of Lion, or cry when Tortoise falls into the river, to be relieved when he turns into a Turtle. Riddle games are also a favourite pastime and two sides may even compete in unravelling these intricate questions. Proverbs are exhanged around the fire and the eager ears of the children pick up the traditional wisdom of the tribe.

On moonlit nights, dancing may entice people away from their fires. Dancing of this kind differs from ritual dancing and is practised mostly by the younger people. The evening is also the time for courting, and many a young man may anoint himself with some sweet-smelling liquid before he sets out to visit a neighbouring village.

As the evening draws on, the activities gradually peter out and the inhabitants retire one by one. The men have a last reassuring look at the cattle and the women see to it that the fires have died down before rolling out the sleeping mats and securing the head rests. The doors are closed tightly and everything is peaceful until dawn.

My father's cattle are all white with a red bull. Teeth and tongue.

My father's goats graze apart on the hill. Ears.

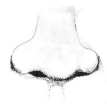

Two holes lead into the anthill. Nostrils.

My father has a little hill which is easily destroyed. His friends come to eat his porridge from his plate.

The blood of the lion is not settled on by flies. Fire.

In the morning, I went crying into the lands. I return in the evening still crying. Brass bangles.

Riddles

In Venda society, riddles are always asked formally and preceded by the word *Thai!* (Riddle). As a rule, short answers of one or two words are accepted, and it is not generally necessary to explain your answer. For instance, the single word *lufheto* (porridge whisk) is as acceptable as the more accurate phase *lufheto lu khalini* (whisk when it is being used to stir the porridge in the pot). If, however, you give an alternative answer that is rarely used, or if you ask a new riddle which nobody knows, you may be asked to explain it before it is accepted as a point in your favour.

A contest begins when someone says 'A ri thaidze!' (Let's ask each other riddles!), and ends when one team can think of no more riddles to ask. The game is played more often by two teams than by two individuals. Boys and girls may play together or on their own, as the occasion arises.

There are two types of riddle-contest, *Thai dza u bulelana* (Riddles that you reveal to each other) and *Thai dza u rengelana* (Riddles that you buy from each other). In team-games, anyone may ask or answer a riddle on behalf of his team at any time. There is no team leader, and players do not have to ask or answer riddles according to any order or precedence. In no single game may the same riddle be asked twice.

Q: My father's beast fell into a pool; I stayed behind and held its tail.
A: Porridge whisk, when it is stirring porridge.

Q: What is an old man whose grey hair is inside his belly?
A: The pumpkin, with its grey fibres inside.

Riddles

When the evening meal is over in the Nyanja society, the children gather round a communal fire in the *'bwalo'* – the cleared space in the middle of the village, or in front of a house – and entertain themselves with songs, folk-stories and riddles.

Anyone may lead off.

'Cilape!' A riddle!

Another child takes up the challenge. *'Nacize!'* Let it come!

The leader then interrogates the rest. The one who answered *'nacize'* has the right to guess first, but should he fail anyone else may attempt the solution. The leader continues to put riddles until one is answered correctly, whereupon they shout *'wafa!'* He has died! Another child (not necessarily the one who guessed the previous riddle) now becomes the interrogator. There is no evidence of splitting up into two groups for riddles as in some societies, though groups are formed in many other play activities.

There does not appear to be any set form of words with which to bring the contest to a close, and the Anyanja say *'atatopa angoleka'* – when they are tired they just stop.

Q: I have many attendants, they have many sleeping mats but they sleep on the ground.

A: Pumpkins. (The leaves of the pumpkin are likened to sleeping mats. The pumpkins are never found resting on the leaves but always on the earth.)

Source: Some riddles of the Nyanja people by Ernest Gray.

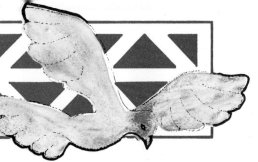

It was in the days of the big hunger. There was a big famine in the land, and Tortoise had no more food left to eat. He walked around the little bushes and hunted, hunted, hunted around for something to put inside his stomach. He hunted, but he found nothing. And so he pulled his head and his little legs under his shell, for he was afraid he might die of hunger.

Now Tortoise is a man who always walks alone. He has no father or mother to take care of him. He has no wife or children who can work for him. So now he would have to die alone, he thought. He lay down with his hungry stomach. *Tu-u-u-u.*

Dove, who sat high up in a tree, saw how Tortoise was hunting for food. She also saw that he found nothing. Nothing at all. And she felt very sorry for him when she saw him lying there so quietly. She sang to him: *Coor-coor, coor-coor,* but he did not put his head out of his shell.

'Tortoise, big man, why don't you go to the other side of the river? I fly there every day, and there is plenty of food.'

Tortoise stuck his head out from under his shell and listened to what Dove had to say.

'Keep quiet, woman!' he shouted. 'How can that food help me if there is a stream of water between me and the food!'

'But you can swim through, big man,' she said.

'I am not a fish that I can swim,' said Tortoise.

'Why don't you fly over the river?'

'Because I am not a bird. Where are my wings?'

Tortoise wept over the plentiful food on the other side of the river. He wept because he was so hungry he was afraid he might die.

Dove wept with him. *Coor-coor, coor-coor, coor-coor!*

Then she had a plan.

'Tortoise,' she said. 'Find a dry stick, and bite on one end.'

'I don't eats sticks, Mother,' said Tortoise sadly.

'It is not for you to eat,' said Dove. 'I will take the other end of the stick in my mouth and fly over the river with you.'

'That is a fine plan, Mother,' said Tortoise.

'Yes, it is a fine plan,' agreed Dove. 'But you must not talk to Fish if he rises from the water to talk to you.'

'No, I will not,' Tortoise promised.

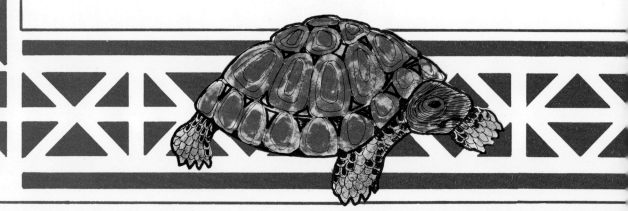

and Dove

And then they did as they had planned. *Yoalo, yoalo.* Tortoise found a dry stick and bit on one end, and Dove bit on the other end, and they flew out over the water. Dove flew over the water, and Tortoise hung below her on the other end of the stick.

Au, but that was a strange business! Fish could not believe what he saw. He looked, he looked, he looked, but he could not understand it at all. He was astonished, for he had never in his life seen a tortoise high up in the sky.

'You, fellow,' said Fish, with his mouth full of water. 'I never knew that you could fly! If I did not see this with my own eyes, I would not have believed it!'

Tortoise became angry with Fish.

'What do you think?' he asked. 'And why should I not be able to fly?'

But before he could finish speaking he fell *twaaah!* right into the water. He had let go of the stick when he argued with Fish, and Dove flew away with only the stick in her mouth.

She came back again to see whether Tortoise would come out of the water. She flew to and fro over the water to see whether Tortoise might come out higher upstream, or whether he might come out of the water lower down. But no, there was no sign of him. She kept on flying, she kept on flying with the stick in her mouth, but to no avail. Tortoise stayed under the water. He did not come up again.

Then she went to lay the little stick down on her nest. But her heart remained black, it would not lie down, because of the big man who had fallen in the water. She wept over him: *Coor-coor, coor-coor . . .*

Every day. Every day. Until this very day.

And she keeps on hunting for Tortoise. She keeps the stick in her mouth. She wants to give it back to Tortoise again so that she can lift him out of the water as soon as he shows his head.

But Tortoise will never come out of the water again. No, he will not, because he found plenty of food under the water on the river bed. Much more food than there ever was on the ground and under the trees. He will never come out of the water again. He will stay there.

And this is how Tortoise became Turtle. And here the story comes to an end.

Source: *Tales from the Basotho* by Minnie Postma.

SERÊLÊLE-SA-TSELA

The name of this game means *Slider of the road.* This name is, as many others, descriptive of the game itself.

Any number of boys and girls can take part. The more players, the more fun, and the better the singing which accompanies the actions. It is one of the few games where boys and girls often play together.

As with most of these games, someone makes the suggestion by saying: *A reng serêlêleng – Let's go serêlêleng.* Each player finds a stone about as big as a tennis ball and they all sit down on their heels to form a circle. The stone is held in the right hand on the ground.

On the command: *Re a thwathwanya fase – We tap on the ground,* the whole crowd start tapping the ground with their stones while singing a song.

The tapping is done to the rhythm of this song, and as soon as the song ends all give the command together: *Re a dikêlêtša – We let go round.* Following this, the stones are passed round the circle. The players pick up the stones and pass them on by putting them down in front of the player on their right-hand side. This is done to the rhythm of the refrain belonging to the song.

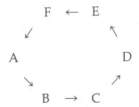

The player must pay careful attention to the rhythm of the song or else a stone will be put in front of him before he is able to move the previous one on to his right-hand neighbour. If this happens that player goes out and thus the circle becomes smaller and smaller until the number of players is too small to carry on. Three players may continue, but when the number is reduced to two the game stops and a new one commences.

Source: H. J. van Zyl, Some of the commonest games played by the Sotho people of Northern Transvaal.

Growing up in a traditional society

The birth of a baby is hailed with great rejoicing by the whole village. The chanting of sacred songs soon fills the air to bring praise to the ancestors for the marvel of new life and perpetuation of the tribe.

The mother of the baby is particularly happy, also because of her economic gain, a woman's wealth being measured by her number of children. No marriage is considered complete until the wife has borne at least one child, thereby honouring the bride-price or *lobola* between her family and that of her husband. The *lobola* usually consists of cattle given to the father of the bride in exchange for the right of the future children to be borne into the family of the groom. The birth of a child also confirms the mother's status as an adult woman in her society.

The baby is given a name on the day when it first appears with its mother in public. The child is often named after an illustrious ancestor, but an important event on the day of the birth or circumstances surrounding the birth can also inspire a name. If a Sotho baby is born on a rainy day, the name *Pula* (rain) may be suitable; or if a Swazi village is enshrouded in mist when the baby arrives, *Ikungu* (mist) may be chosen. The names are sometimes changed during the initiation ritual when the children come of age, like in Xhosa society.

The ceremonies welcoming the baby usually include the slaughtering of a goat, not only in preparation of a feast of thanksgiving to the ancestors but also to obtain a soft skin to use as a blanket for the baby. Among the Nguni this goat is known as the *imbeleko* goat, from *ukubeleka*, the term for carrying the child on the back. In the ensuing months, mother and baby are inseparable as she constantly carries the infant tied to her back in the soft skin. In this secure position, the baby accompanies the mother wherever she goes, rocking to and fro with the movement of her body when she grinds corn or bouncing up and down to the rhythm of a traditional dance.

After a few months, the baby is entrusted to the care of a small girl, usually an older sister or a cousin. These young nurses gather together with their charges and the baby is thus part of a group of his or her peers from an early age. This group is always closely knit, and the child is never lonely and never lacks playmates.

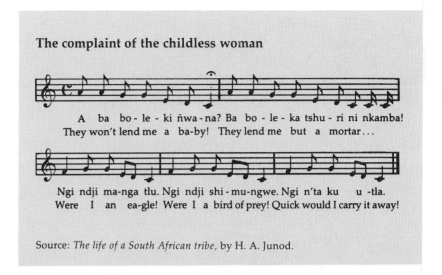

The complaint of the childless woman

A ba bo - le - ki ñwa - na? Ba bo - le - ka tshu - ri ni nkamba!
They won't lend me a ba-by! They lend me but a mortar...

Ngi ndji ma-nga tlu. Ngi ndji shi - mu-ngwe. Ngi n'ta ku u -tla.
Were I an ea-gle! Were I a bird of prey! Quick would I carry it away!

Source: *The life of a South African tribe,* by H. A. Junod.

Children are weaned between the ages of one and three years. Weaning ends the period of babyhood; the toddlers romp and frolic together while all the women take an interest in their well-being. The child is regarded as belonging to the group and if a mother should be overly strict or careless in the treatment of her child, the older women would admonish her. A tribesman commented thus on this communal concern with a child: 'On the fateful day when the baby takes its first step, there are more women than I have fingers and toes to admire it, applaud and prevent it from toppling.'

Under so many watchful eyes, the toddlers are quite safe and only three rules are enforced: children must not play with fire or with knives, and they must always show respect for others, especially their elders.

The rule of showing respect to others is an essential part of the upbringing of a child in traditional society. Training of the child concerns the acquisition of social skills in compliance with the traditional way of life. The future role of the child is prescribed by its sex, its position in the family and its parents' place in society. In the words of Virginia van der Vliet: 'In essence, the problems of socializing the human infant are universal – the child must be taught to accept, value and reproduce the behaviour and sentiments of the society into which he is born.'

Some of the customs which children must obey are the correct way of greeting their elders of both sexes by raising the hand and addressing them by their names, to clap hands before receiving a gift, to share things unselfishly, especially food, and to wait for their turn to eat and not show greediness.

Another important phase in the life cycle is marked when the toddler loses the two first front teeth (called *ukukhumka* by the Xhosa). The carefree years of infancy have then come to an end, and boys and girls are separated to be introduced to the customary tasks of society. During the following two years the small boys gain experience by herding the less valuable stock: their fathers' goats and calves. The small girls are trained in housekeeping by assisting their mothers with household chores, and in infant care by looking after a small brother or sister.

At the age of approximately ten the boys start herding the cattle under the critical eyes of the older herd boys until they can take full responsibility. The herd boys form a subculture of their own in the society. Leadership is often established by means of 'stickfighting', a skill they practise from an early age. The days in the veld are filled with exciting activities like hunting rabbits or other small game, even killing birds on the wing by accurately hurling a wooden club, by robbing birds' nests, roasting insects, fashioning clay oxen or bathing and romping in the shallows.

The girls do not learn as much of the veldlore as the boys do, but they become well versed in the gathering of veld foods like the various edible leafy vegetables, wild fruit or bulbs available near the village. They are also taught the numerous household duties, often through play. A girl will have her own miniature calabash and clay pot and balance them on her head, emulating her elders. When she accompanies her mother to the fields she has her own small hoe to practise agricultural tasks.

The children play various games, and in some Sotho and Venda groups miniature villages evolve under the supervision of the elders, where children play at being grown-up, cooking, grinding and hunting just as they have seen their elders do. This role also affords valuable training for duties in later life.

With puberty comes sexual maturity, and this marks the introduction into adulthood. When a young girl starts menstruating it is made public, because she is ready for initiation into adulthood. In some communities advent of menstruation of a girl is celebrated with a ceremony; the Zulu prepares a temporary drum, an *ingungu*, for this occasion by securing a goatskin over a clay beer pot.

Amongst some tribes a number of adolescents of the same sex go through initiation ceremonies together. These puberty rites differ between communities, but the objectives are more or less the same. An old man described them as follows: 'Children in puberty, like newly dried jackal pelts, need to be softened and fashioned by their wiser elders, for otherwise they turn out hard and unpliable and inadequate.' Initiation lodges are built usually after the crops have been harvested in autumn, and the rites continue until the first rains fall in spring. In some communities the young men are circumcised during initiation, and instruction is given in traditions and sexual matters. This period marks the introduction of the young people into adulthood and concludes the childhood years.

The herd boys form a subculture of their own in society. Leadership is often established by means of stickfighting

Courtesy, hospitality and etiquette

Courtesy training starts early in childhood and from the beginning politeness to others and obedience to elders are inculcated. Hospitality and etiquette are stressed throughout life and correct behaviour, generosity and willingness to share are heavily emphasized in childhood. Teaching children how to live in peace with other members of the community, which is a basis of sound adult relationships, is subtly woven into childrearing practices.

The Black man thoroughly understands and practises the laws of hospitality in the most generous manner. The stranger is always made welcome, and given every assistance possible, but both visitor and host must observe the correct etiquette practices according to their customs.

When a visitor approaches a village he is expected to wait outside the village gate until a messenger is sent out to accompany him to the village council-place. The visitor will show his respect by bowing down to the chief or headman and seat himself just inside the entrance. The chief will then formally question him about the purpose of his visit and ask him whether he wishes to stay over. If so, a hut is prepared for the visitor and he is offered beer and food.

The visitor is expected to leave his weapons outside the village gate and these will be brought to him once it has been established that the purpose of the visit is peaceful. The mode of conversation is very formal: a messenger quite often acts as mouthpiece and conveys messages between the visitor and host although they can both hear clearly what is being said. When the introductory proceedings are concluded the messenger leaves. Exchange of news is eagerly sought after but this too is done in a prescribed fashion. Among the Tsonga a special mat is rolled out to seat the visitor and host for this conversation. The visitor relates his news in a chanting tone and the host interrupts with *Ahina, ahina,* that is 'Indeed, indeed'. After the narration is completed, the rest of the audience exclaims *Hina!* – a hearty 'Thank you'. Then the master of the village relates his news in the same tone. There is often an exchange of tobacco or snuff at this stage, which is always regarded as a friendly gesture.

In most societies women visitors are usually escorted to the courtyard of the main wife of the chief, but if she has to convey her news

The eagle which seizes is the one which has hovered above – one will only get something by working diligently for it.

The perspiration of the dog is absorbed in his hair – a man's hard work is often not apparent to others.

The polecat cannot smell himself – a man cannot see his own faults.

Baboons laugh at each other's deep-set eyes – a man will criticise in others the faults which he has himself.

A conceited person is like the throat of a frog – puffed up and full of wind.

to the men at the council-place, she is supposed to sit down before talking to the men, a sign of respect. A girl who has not yet reached puberty kneels down with body erect and says why she is sent, while a very old woman may stand, as long as she bends her body forward, resting both hands on her knees.

The rules for relatives visiting the village are not as formal but are observed carefully. If the grandfather, for example, pays a visit his son or grandson runs to meet him at the village gate and carries his club. He is escorted to the homestead and seated in the visitor's place. The son welcomes his father, using the family name in addressing him. The wife then greets the visitor and he replies using her family name. Some small talk about the weather is followed by the son asking about his father's well-being, how things are at his village and how long he will be staying. The old man is not interrupted and only when he is finished are questions asked. The son then tells him his news.

A female visitor, such as the grandmother or aunt, is given the same cordial reception as the grandfather. She is received in the same way, but the wife must also be present at the formal welcoming. When the visitor departs, she is given a basket of millet or a portion of meat to take back to her village as a token of the host's hospitality. The head of the family and his wife walk with her a little way along the road before bidding her farewell.

Family relations are very important in traditional society and a number of courtesy and etiquette rules are woven into the kinship

pattern of the family. A child is taught the correct behaviour towards different relatives according to the child's position in the family. Age is an important status position in this society and respect is shown to all elderly people. All people older than the child are held in deference and particularly first-born brothers and sisters have special status and privileges.

The brothers and sisters of the father and mother are considered to be additional 'fathers' and 'mothers', but their status alters according to age. The eldest paternal 'uncle' will be more highly respected and will have a name depicting honour. In some societies these 'fathers' and 'mothers' have specified responsibilities towards their nieces and nephews and a special relationship develops between child and relative, particularly when the latter is the mother's brother.

The grandparents have a warm, sound relationship with the child and tend to spoil their grandchildren. In some societies the child lives with the maternal grandparents for a time and this has given rise to the expression in the Zulu society for a spoilt child: 'This child must have grown up among his (her) mother's people.'

The grandmothers, both paternal and maternal, are treated with great respect by the mother, and the child regards them as the 'chief women'.

The respect for age induces a sense of humility in the people, and has great value in the society. Traditional society has a keen sense of duty regarding the care of the aged.

Strict etiquette rules are also observed with food service and at meal times. Children are taught from infancy not to be greedy and to share food. They must never show that they are hungry and may not gulp down food, but should wait their turn and eat slowly and with decorum. The child may not take food from the pot but must receive it in both hands, as are all other gifts. The child is discouraged from asking for food other than from the mother, and children are rebuked for straying into other homesteads at mealtimes where hospitality rules would force the woman of the home to offer them food.

At mealtimes food is usually dished into communal containers and groups of children of the same sex but of different ages would share a plate. The girls who have reached puberty usually share a plate with the mother while older boys have their own container or share with the father.

The main cereal dish is served in a clay, wooden, calabash or basketry container and the side dish of vegetable, meat or other relish in a smaller container. These containers are placed on mats in the homestead or in the courtyard. The proper way for women to sit on these mats is to swing their legs to the side and rest one hand on the mat to support the body. Boys are taught to sit with their legs crossed. It is considered rude to stand while eating or to walk about during the meal.

Everyone wash their hands before the meal and eating is done with the fingers. Only the tips of the fingers are used and a piece of food is broken off with the thumb and first finger of the right hand. It

is swiftly rolled into a rounded shape with the help of the other fingers of the same hand. The tip of the morsel is then dipped into the side dish, and care is taken that the fingers do not touch the food in the container; the morsel is then popped into the mouth with a deft movement. No piece of food may be dipped twice.

In the case of a meat dish, the procedure is to take a portion with the right hand and transfer it to the palm of the left. A piece of the cereal dish is taken with the right hand in the usual way, dipped into the gravy of the meat, put into the mouth and immediately afterwards the piece of meat is placed into the mouth with the left hand.

Food is always eaten decorously and slowly. These neat mannerisms in partaking of food must rank this tradition among the most attractive eating customs in the world. When a soft food is served, everybody is provided with a homemade spoon.

The men and older boys receive their morning meal at the council-place or wherever they are occupied. Their food is usually placed in individual containers and either conveyed in lidded baskets or covered with clay lids. Water for washing hands and rinsing the mouth is sent along. When a man receives the food with both hands, no verbal thanks need be expressed. Younger men have to wait for their elders to start the meal before they do, and they may not leave the council-place while their elders are still eating.

Guests are served considerably more food than they are expected to eat and it is etiquette to leave some in the dish to indicate that they have been satisfied.

When the meal is served in the homestead, guests and family members must observe etiquette concerning seating position. The accompanying sketch indicates the seating arrangement in the Swazi *umzi*.

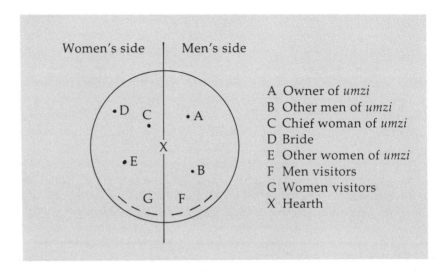

A special, obscure seat is indicated for the bride as she has to observe various special etiquette rules.

When she arrives in the village of her husband, she is already well versed in agricultural practices as well as in cooking, but she is equally well trained in rules pertaining to etiquette. For the first few months she plays a very subordinate role to her mother-in-law and other members of the new family. While not revealing any of her capabilities, she spends her time learning from them about the traditions of their village. She gradually obtains more status until eventually she possesses her own hearth, cooking pots and other utensils, her own fields and granaries, and oversees the preparation of food in her homestead. The husband sometimes asks for a special dish but the wife usually decides on the menu and he unconditionally accepts her choice.

Swazi bride

Foods

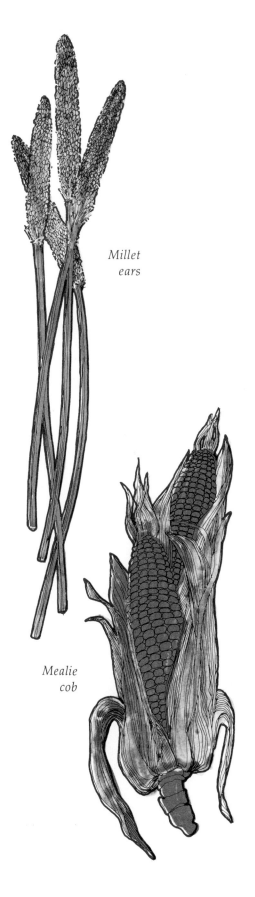

Millet
ears

Food production

Food production and food preparation are the responsibility (and privilege) of the wife in a traditional society. She is the agriculturalist and has her own field or garden for the production of food for her own household.

Agriculture has been practised in southern Africa for many centuries. Excavations near the Limpopo River revealed melon pips and sorghum seeds, traced by means of the carbon-dating method to the 11th century.

The earliest written records of agriculture south of the Limpopo came from shipwrecked sailors who explored the coastal regions in 1554 and reported that they 'stole a large basket of millet' to sustain themselves. The millet mentioned by the sailors is indigenous to tropical Africa and Asia. The grasslike plants bear short ears filled with fine seeds, and today several groups still cherish this plant for its beer-making qualities. For very special occasions beer is made from millet. (It is not produced on a large scale, as it does not yield large crops.) Finger millet *(Eleusine corocana)* and pearl millet *(Pennisetum typhoideum)* are the two most popular varieties.

Other crops were also noted in old records and maize, melons, beans, gourds and sugarcane were part of the diet mentioned by sailors in 1635.

Maize, also called Indian or Turkish corn in old documents, was introduced to southern Africa via Central Africa from Central America. According to linguists, the term maize is derived from *ma'hiz*, an Arawak word used in South America and the West Indies. The term used in southern Africa is mealie, which is derived from *milho*, the Portuguese word for sorghum. The maize plant was first introduced to western Africa by Portuguese navigators and it soon replaced the indigenous cereal crop of sorghum, called *milho*. The new crop also became known as *milho* and although the name maize was used in Europe, the name *mily* was used in old documents in southern Africa. The botanical name of the plant is *Zea mays*. Among the Zulu and Swazi it is known as *umbila* and the Sotho names are *poone*, while the Pedi call it *mmidi*, the Venda *mavhele* and the Xhosa *umbona*.

Mealie
cob

A variety of dishes are made from maize, but the most popular dish is porridge in its numerous forms.

A variety of some 20 maize porridges are made in southern Africa, the textures of which may vary from dry and crumbly to soft and runny. The latter may be artistically served in the form of a sculptured pyramid. The maize is ground to varying degrees of fineness as required for particular dishes.

Sorghum is still cultivated today and is indigenous to Africa. An Egyptian mural in the tomb of Amenemes dating back to 2200 BC, depicts sorghum plants, which indicate this plant's centuries-long affiliation with Africa. According to the late Professor F. X. Laubscher, a renowned plant geneticist, *sorghum* is the botanical name for a family of grasses and he speculates that their cultivation probably started in Central Africa. A variety of different sorghums are cultivated south of the Limpopo; the Pedi, for example, grow six different kinds. *Motleriane* var. is popularly used for beer as well as porridge, but the red seeds are equally sought after by the finches which swarm to the fields when the ears ripen. *Morolong* var. does not attract finches but the white seeds are likewise not too palatable as food for humans. For beer production *Malahlwane* var. is excellent, and has the advantage that its grey seeds do not attract the birds. The other three varieties used by the Pedi are all 'finch proof' and are also acceptable for use as porridge and in beer making.

Sorghum ears

The popular name for sorghum is *amabele* in most southern African languages. It is also known as *amazimba* in Xhosa and *luvhele* in Venda. Various dishes are made from *amabele* but its use in beer making is considered the most important.

One variety of sorghum, *Sorghum brot,* known as sweet cane or *imfe* amongst the Zulu and as *nyoba* among the Pedi, is planted and eaten as a snack for its sweet taste. This plant is presumably the 'sugar cane' mentioned in old records.

The 'large melons which are very good' mentioned in these records are also indigenous to Africa. Of the family *Citrullus lanatus*, various kinds are found in Africa and two are included in the Pedi diet, the *morotse* (citron or maketaan) and the *mogapu* (watermelon with yellow flesh). Varieties eaten by other groups do not differ much from these two. The Sotho name for the melon is *lerôtse*, the Zulu call it *ibece*, the Venda *gwabi*, the Ndebele *ljodo* and the Shangana *gwembe*.

These melons are a popular crop because they are resistant to drought and can be stored for long periods of time. A variety of dishes are prepared from the flesh, but a delectable stewed dish is made from the young tendrils and fruits and the seeds are considered a delicacy when fried and served with porridge. The fresh melon is eaten as is, and many a weary traveller has gleefully quenched his thirst on the juicy pulp of a melon.

The gourds mentioned by the shipwrecked sailors are indigenous to tropical Africa and many different varieties have developed through natural propagation. Botanically the plants are known as *Lagenaria siceraria*. The edible kinds are usually those with a rough skin, but a dish is prepared of the young fruits and leaves of all kinds, the taste being comparable to that of mushrooms. Gourds are cultivated mostly for making eating vessels and other household containers. These plants are called *liselwa* or *iselwa* by the Swazi, *amaselwa* by the Zulu, *moraka* by the Pedi, *uselwa* by the Xhosa, *seho* by the Sotho and *zwitemba* by the Venda.

Edible mopani worm

It is interesting to note that beans were encountered by early travellers. The traditional diet was therefore nutritious according to modern standards, as beans have a high protein content. The beans indigenous to Africa are the jugobean (*Voandzeia subterranea*) and cowpea (*Vigna unguiculata*). Although of Indian origin, the mungbean (*Vigna radiata*) is also cultivated extensively and has been planted in Africa from time immemorial. The jugobean bears its fruit underground in a pod, while the cowpea bears its pod above the ground – but interestingly, it is not a pea but a bean. All these legumes are used in a number of traditional dishes. In addition their leaves are also used as food and prepared as green stews or cooked with cereal.

A later addition to the African menu is the groundnut or monkeynut (*Arachis hypogaea*) which is cultivated mainly in the northern, eastern and central parts of South Africa and enhances many traditional dishes.

The pumpkin (*Cucurbita* spp.) came to Africa from the Americas. It has been accepted in traditional cooking and is often honoured in traditional ceremonies. Through natural mutation of the original species, a great variety of pumpkins are grown in different areas. It is prepared in many different ways – as a vegetable, mixed with cereal, as a porridge; the young fruits are stewed; a delicious dish is prepared from the flowers and the seeds are fried and served with porridge.

Meat and milk

The provision of meat and milk is the contribution of the menfolk to the food supply. Looking after the cattle and goats is the responsibility of the male, who is also the owner, and from a young age boys are taught to work with animals. The herd boys milk the cows and when the wooden milking pails are full they pour the milk into calabashes or into leather milk sacks to curdle. Curds, called *amasi* by the Zulu and Xhosa and *mafi* by the Sotho, is a favourite dish and in old documents reference is made to the enjoyment Black people have in consuming curds. Fresh milk is given only to babies or the very old and infirm.

Chickens, pigs and sheep were relatively recently introduced into Africa and did not form part of the traditional diet.

Meat is traditionally 'only a visitor' in the diet, to use the Pedi vernacular. Cattle have a prominent place in traditional society as the principal medium of exchange and the 'currency' in which court fines are paid. Cattle is the most common means of obtaining a wife, through payment of a bride-price to the girl's family. Ritual ceremonies and social festivities are also dependent on cattle either for ritual sacrifices or for family or traditional feasts. The possession of cattle thus gives social importance to the owner, and slaughter of these animals merely for food hardly ever occurs.

If, however, an animal is slaughtered, tradition has to be observed in the whole procedure. In the Bavenda society a man is selected to kill the animal with a single thrust of the assegai through its heart. The blood is collected for traditional dishes and the lips and cheeks are immediately cut off and fried. Next the skin of the tail is removed, and is treasured as a cover for clubs or assegais. The different limbs and parts are then divided among the various participants according

Milk poured through gourd 'funnel' into calabash bound with mopani bark and palm leaves

to custom. The whole carcass is disposed of, leaving the host with only his appointed portion.

Although stock is rarely slaughtered, the people are fond of meat, and game and birds were often eaten in the times when wild animals still abounded.

Hunting and food gathering

The principal weapons employed in the hunt are, as in warfare, the spear, the axe and the club. Only the Venda make use of the bow and arrow. Hunting parties are usually organised and large animals such as hippopotami, elephants or rhinoceros were stalked or trapped in pits. The division of the carcass is again prescribed by tradition and the whole carcass is disposed of on the same day.

Some animals are considered unfit for consumption in some communities as a result of taboos and certain totem animals are never killed.

Small-game hunting, like hares or hedgehogs or birds, is the sport of the herd boys, whose weapon is a club flung with great accuracy. They also set traps or construct snares for these animals. Most boys know the use of bird lime, and spread the sticky plant material on the resting place of birds, whereupon the birds cannot free themselves and are caught by hand. Field mice are also trapped and eaten roasted as special titbits.

Fishing

Fishing is not widely practised since most people regard fish as akin to snakes.

The Tsonga, however, relish fish and the women catch fish with conical basket traps especially made for this purpose. The traps are pushed around in shallow river water or pools and any fish caught are removed through a hole in the top of the basket.

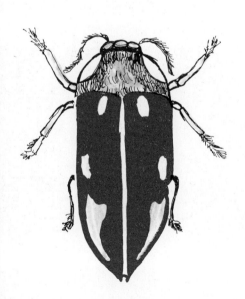

Herd boys of most societies often while away their time by shooting fish in shallow water with bow and arrow. At the coast, Xhosa men spear fish in shallow pools. The women living near the coast collect shellfish, and at low tide cockles *(Turbo sarmaticus)*, limpets *(Patella tabularis)*, periwinkles *(Oxystele sinesis)*, Venus ears *(Haliotis midae)*, oysters *(Crassostreae* sp.), redbait *(Pyura stolonifera)*, pink lady *(Charonia pustulata)* and mussels *(Mtilus perna)* are collected. In eastern Pondoland crayfish is also collected by women and youths.

The empty shells are used in various ways: limpet shells serve as spoons to feed babies or as pot scrapers, and the large snail shell of the *Achatina* sp. is often used as a baby bottle.

Insects

Another source of protein is provided by insects gathered in great masses by most societies. Numerous kinds are collected and are very popular foods.

Different kinds of locusts are collected during the night after a swarm has settled. When the insects are asleep, they are gathered by the handful from the shrubs and trees and placed into large bags or baskets.

◁ 9 The colourful designs of a Ndebele
village

◁ 10 Construction of Zulu hut, showing sapling poles for frame, grass for thatching, and grass ropes to tie grass to the roof

11 Veld foods

The traditional diet was richly enhanced with foods gathered in the veld. Three baskets full were collected near a Venda village:

Top left:
Vegetable basket with purple-green *maroho (Amaranthus hybridus L.)* and dried marula *(Schlerocarya caffra).*

Top right:
Insect basket with dried marula worms, grasshoppers and ants.

Large basket:
Veld fruit, clockwise from the top: Two ripe marulas; marula pips to be cracked for their nuts; *muhatu (Tabernaemontana elegans); munii –* with a date-like taste *(Berchemia discolor); muhuyu-ngala* (wild figs) *(Ficus capensis); mutuhu (Trichilia emetica);* boabab *(Adansonia digitata)* fruit. In the centre are large green *murambas (Strychnos spinosa).*

◁ **12 Milk**

Milk is more than a food in traditional
African society. Kinship is indicated
by partaking of milk from a specific
herd, and in some communities milk
is sprinkled in the home for
purification after a death has occured.
Curds (*amasi/masi/mafi*) is used in the
various traditional dishes and only the
very young and very old drink fresh
milk.

A wooden milk pail, milk
calabashes and drinking calabashes
are displayed.

13 Meat storage

In the Zulu community a special ledge
is built inside a hut and all meat
products are kept there. In the Zulu
community wooden dishes and
wooden spoons are used for serving
and storing meat and special mats are
woven to cover raw meat.

The liver and meat sausage in the
chitterling is very tasty when roasted
over coals. It is displayed in the
foreground with the raw ingredients
on a wooden spoon at the back.
Pigeons baked in clay under the coals
are stacked on a wooden dish, ready to
be broken open and served.

◁ **14 Barbeque**

The only dish prepared by men in traditional society was barbequed beef on spits for special occasions. This was served with beer and often honey in the comb.

Against the backdrop of the cattle fold in the Zulu village, the beer-brewing pot, beer strainer, beer-serving calabash and various beer-drinking pots covered with basketry lids are ready for the feast. Honey combs are stacked on a wooden dish and celebrations will commence as soon as the meat is seared.

◁ **15 Beer brewing and serving utensils**

Traditional beer made from sorghum, millet and, more recently, mealies, is deeply interwoven with African cultural life. At traditional festivities like rain-making ceremonies, 'first-fruit' festivities and religious offerings, the most decorative pots and utensils were used to serve the beer.

Note the millet and sorghum ears in the background, the plaited beer sieves, traditional beer stirrer and skimmer spoon and the Zulu beer basket and container. Men sat on tree stumps and women on grass mats. Some of the small, decorated 'party-ware' drinking pots are filled to the brim with sorghum beer.

◁ 16 Beverages

In traditional society several beverages are prepared.

Top: Ilala palm beer (with *ilala* palm-leaf beer strainer).
Centre: Amahewu/mahleu (with mealie ear).
Anticlockwise, from left: Marula beer (with fresh marulas); wild honey beer (with honey in comb); sorghum and millet beer (with sorghum and millet ears).

Flying ants or termites are also considered a delicacy. In the summer before the rain falls, these ants emerge from their underground dwellings and fly some distance before shedding their wings. The ants are either collected then, or their dwellings are opened up and the termites collected.

Caterpillars are usually collected when they are fully grown and swollen from feeding on the leaves of trees. Different kinds of caterpillars are eaten, but those feeding on the mopane tree *(Colophospermum mopane)* are probably preferred as a delicacy.

Sand crickets appear in the rainy season, and their presence is recognised by a small heap of soil on the ground. This heap is opened up with a stick or hoe and the crickets are caught. In season hundreds can be collected in a day.

Certain kinds of beetles feeding on leaves of trees, some having an irritating buzz in the summer months, are also collected. Their hard outer wings and legs are removed when they are taken off the trees and the remainder of their bodies is put in baskets.

Bees contribute a delicacy to the diet in the form of honey. Different kinds of wild bees are indigenous to Africa and quite often people are led to a nest by the honey bird. The bird gives a peculiar call and when followed moves on to a tree some distance away. This procedure is repeated until the nest is reached, where the bird is rewarded with a portion of the honey. The bees are smoked out, the combs removed and placed in a container, usually on a piece of bark. The honey that is not eaten on the spot is taken home and squeezed out into a container to be eaten with a spoon as a special sweet.

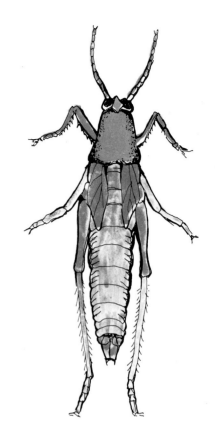

Plant food from the veld

Collected plant food add considerably to the variety of the diet. From an early age girls accompany their mothers and aunts to collect veld foods, and are taught which plants are edible. Different sections of the plants are used as food depending on the type of plant, and bulbs, roots, shoots, seeds, flowers, fruits or leaves are eaten. The species eaten by the various tribes are numerous, and in Lesotho alone the botanist Jacot-Guillarmod listed 88 different plants used as food.

The best-known plantfood dish is prepared from the leaves of a variety of plants and the dish is called *morogo* or *imifino* by different language groups. It is often called 'women's food', indicating their partiality to the food and that the men do not consider it filling enough as a food. The plants most commonly used for this dish are:

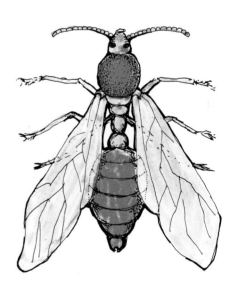

Pigweed – *Amaranthus deflexus*
Blackjack – *Bidens pilosa*
Postelein – *Portulaca oleracea*
Nightshade – *Solanum nigrum*
Lamb's-quarters – *Chenopodium album, C. murale, C. ambrosioides, C. bontei, C. multifidum*
Cape gooseberry – *Physalis angulata*
Sow-thistle – *Sonchus oleraceus*
Nettle – *Urtica dioica, U. urens*
Cowpea – *Vigna unguiculata*
Pumpkin tops – *Cucurbita* spp.
Wild spinach – *Gynandropsis gynandra*

According to Dr Fox, who has been doing research on these edible plants for almost 50 years, leaves for this dish are gathered from numerous plants – the Zulu use the leaves of more than a hundred different plants.

When wild fruits are in season, they are also included in the diet. More than 70 varieties are eaten in southern Africa. The following are some of the favourite fruits eaten by the Pedi: *mohlono* (kei-apple) *(Dovyalis caffra)*, a small, apricot-like tangy fruit; *mimilo* (wild medlar) *(Vangueria infausta)*, brown fruits with a mealy texture; *ditshid* (sour plum) *(Ximenia caffra)*, small yellow-red plums with a tangy taste (the pips have a high fat content, and when ground are used as a cosmetic); *motlatswa* (stem fruit or wild plum) *(Bequartiodendron Magalies montanum)*, small fruits with a taste reminiscent of litchis (the small trees bear a lot of fruit – as much as 80 kg may be collected); *morotlue* (wild orange or monkey apple) *(Strychnos pugens)*, the ripe fruit look like an orange, but the skin is very hard.

The small marula *(Sclerocarya caffra)* fruits are tasty and the stones are eaten as a delicacy. The marula tree is of majestic size and bears profusely.

These deciduous wild fruits are often preserved by drying them in the sun. The fruit is pounded in the mortar and shaped into patties.

Another impressive wild fruit tree is the baobab *(Adansonia digitata)*, probably the largest tree in Africa to attain a great age, often a few centuries. The fruits are large, measuring up to about 35 cm in length and 20 cm in width. The inside of the fruit has a sponge-like texture and is rather like flour. It has a pleasant acid taste and is often roasted, or else mixed with maize, millet, sorghum or milk to make a porridge.

Although the number of traditional crops appears to be limited, the women are very resourceful in using these ingredients. Different dishes have evolved, and with these a palate very discerning as to the right taste of the dishes. For example, the Pedi boasts the following selection of traditional dishes, made from the crops of the field:

Cereal (flour) dishes – 48
Whole cereal dishes – 13
Cereal leaf dishes – 30
Roasted seeds – 4
Bean relishes – 3
Bean dishes – 3

If the wild foods collected near the village are included, the list is further extended:

Wild fruit relishes – 2
Fruit and vegetable dishes – 20
Insect dishes – 13
Beverages – 12

Adding to the above the occasional meat dish, the woman in traditional society thus offers quite a variation of dishes to her family.

Harvesting, threshing, milling

The first fruits of the new year ripen towards the middle of summer. Green mealies, new sorghum, sweet cane, tender young beans and the first pumpkins and melons usually tempt the palate before the 'first fruits ceremony' is conducted. This event signals the sanction of the ancestral spirits to enjoy the season's new crops.

For the following three months the people revel in the fresh foods as relief from the dry staple cereal diet of the last winter days. When the crops have ripened fully the harvest season starts.

The agricultural year ends with the harvesting of the grain crops, by which time the vegetable crops have already been stored away for winter. All available hands are expected at the fields where the mealie and sorghum ears are picked and thrown in heaps at the edge of the fields. At night the day's collection is conveyed home in baskets or on ox-drawn sledges.

At the village the ears of grain are dried on specially made mud platforms, on constructed wooden frames or on flat rock out-croppings. The sheaths of the mealie cobs are often drawn back and tied together to hang in bundles from ceilings or drying racks.

People usually have more leisure time after the harvest, and as a result of the abundant new grain, beer is plentiful. Spirits are high and this is the great festive season; weddings, initiations and other celebrations are conducted and there is much informal visiting and entertainment.

Although harvesting is done, threshing still remains, and this activity is undertaken in a leisurely way throughout the festive season.

The threshing procedures differ in different communities, but a threshing floor is always necessary. For millet or sorghum a threshing floor is prepared from mud, creating a hard, clean surface, or a hut is swept clean for this purpose. The ears of corn are stacked in the middle of the floor and beaten with flails which are either clubs or sticks, according to custom. Usually large flails are made for adults and smaller ones for young girls. Mealies may also be threshed in this way, but more often the seeds are rubbed from the cob by hand. This shelling is done while people sit around the cob heap, conversing happily or chanting a song.

Some of the best grain is saved for seed for the next planting season and the rest is stored in granaries. These granaries vary and huts with basketry and pottery containers or platforms with storage containers or underground pits are most commonly used. Protection against weevils is attempted by constructing airtight containers or storage pits or by pouring the ash of burnt aloe leaves over the grain.

Preparing grain for the traditional dishes is a tedious task performed almost daily by the womenfolk. The upright posture and good shape of tribal women can be attributed to the regular exercise obtained while working at the pounding block or the grinding stone and are further enhanced by balancing loads on their heads.

When a mealie dish is to be prepared, mealies are fetched from the granary and taken to the pounding block in a carrying basket. The wooden receptable, made from a tree trunk, is filled one third with mealies, and water is sprinkled to dampen the grain. The pestle, roughly 1,2 m in length, is used with regular strokes, with pauses in between for adding water to soften the husks. This process is continued until all the mealies are pounded to the required size. It is transferred to the winnowing basket, a shallow, traylike basket with rounded sides and roughly 70 cm in diameter. The basket is swirled from side to side to separate the grain and husks, and shaken lightly in the wind for the husks to be winnowed.

This grain has to go through a further process on the grinding stone if meal is to be prepared. The mill or grinding stone has been in use for many centuries in Africa and Egyptian women of old used grinding stones in the same way as do the tribal women in the southern part of the continent. The grinding stone consists of two parts, a flat, receptacle stone to hold the grain and a rounded, oblong stone used to crush the grain with a to-and-fro motion.

The Tsonga woman places the lower grinding stone, called *guyo*, on three supporting foundation stones to create a slight slope. She kneels down behind the higher edge and places the shallow winnowing basket beneath the lower edge to catch the meal. Her rolling stone is called *huyo*.

The Sotho woman uses a flat stone with a slight indentation, called *lelwala*, as a bottom stone and grinds the grain with a cylindrical *tsilo*. The meal is swept with a small broom on to a tightly woven grass mat.

In the Xhosa community, the grinding stone is placed on a clay pedestal in the back of the kitchen hut.

The Pedi women share a communal grinding stone. It is a flat rock outcropping near the village and each woman has her own rolling stone which she hides in the shrubs nearby. A watchman guards the stone during the night to protect it from any evildoers and only leaves in the morning after the first woman has come to grind.

The art of producing the correct grind for every traditional dish is held in great esteem in tribal culture. The ground meal is winnowed and returned to the grinding stone until the desired fineness is obtained. Girls are taught very early what the required meal qualities are, and a serious reprimand from a mother to a daughter is 'you grind carelessly'!

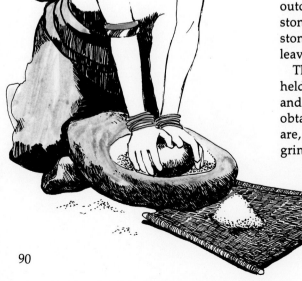

⋂ame of month, productive cycle and food cycle

(according to Hilda Beemer)

Month (English and approximate Swazi equivalent)	*Productive cycle*	*Food cycle*
January *(Bimbitwane):* Everyone is satisfied	Last month possible for planting maize in areas where there is no frost. Last gardens, known as *sangcapa*. People getting ready to protect the corn from birds.	Slight rains, plenty of food – new mealies, pumpkins, gourds, sugar cane. Fruit on trees ripen – incosi, etc., sorghum ripening. Marula beer.

AUTUMN (LIKWINDLA)

February *(Indlovana):* Little elephant	Bringing in new mealies from early gardens. Women and children very busy guarding sorghum, weeding the last gardens. Men break up old and virgin fields and allow them to lie unworked during winter.	Slight rain. Still eating new mealies and fresh foods and vegetables; cow peas and ground nuts ripen. Women begin to bring in sorghum. Marula beer.
March *(Indlovu enkulu):* Big elephant	Still bringing in mealies and legumes. Early burning of grazing fields.	New mealies and legumes. Marula beer.

WINTER (UBUSIKA)

April (*Mabasa*): Everyone begins to make a fire (*kubasa*). Beginning of cold season

Dry maize and fresh corn reaped, grain platforms built for storing old mealies. Women tie the bundles of mealies together in the fields. Work sporadically from early in the morning until late in the afternoon.

Mealies getting dry, corn and the making of beer, greens at an end, using of dried vegetables. Milk getting scarce.

May (*Inkwekweti*): To pick up everything you have (*kwekweta*)

Harvest dry mealies for storage, picking corn, bringing in last pumpkins. Some peasants turning the grounds for next sowing. Hunting. Cattle graze in harvested fields.

Unusual for it to rain. Greens already old and bitter. Using dry mealies. Cows milked only once a day.

May to June (*Inhlangula kuhlangula emancembe*): To brush off the leaves

Beans and maize from last maize gardens are reaped. Women busy cutting grass for the huts, mats and baskets. Men cut saplings. Burning of late garden sites. Women and men busy with building material. Hunts arranged.

Strong north winds and leaves blown about. No rain. Start on stored foods. Beer drinks from first sorghum and eat boiled whole corn. Very little milk. Dried greens. *Emahaia* (*Aloe* sp.) begins to flower; eat its root.

July (*Kolwane*): A hawk, *kolwane*, which nests during this month

End of harvest, ploughing but no planting. Waiting for spring rains. Hunting season. Cutting of grass, etc., for building. Cleaning and threshing of corn. Mealies ripe for storing. Beans and peas brought in.

Little rain. Old food as above. Beer drinks on newly ripe. Cereals, beans, sorghum, peas and pumpkins. Hunting season.

SPRING (EMAHLOBOLUTUNDLANA)

August *(Inci)*

If rain falls early gardens are planted with mealies, pumpkins, potatoes and sugar cane. Corn ripens in the fields for storage. Planting started in high lands. Busy burning grass.

Little rain. Food still sufficient in store huts. Cattle show slight improvement in quantity of milk given. Palm wine.

September *(Inyoni):* A bird Inyoni named Phezukwomkono mates

Very busy ploughing, planting and weeding and trying to finish off huts before heavy rains set in. Planting beans and peas as well as maize, etc.

Early rains. Mealies getting less. Few greens and mushrooms. Using sorghum.

October *(Impala):* The antelope impala gives birth during this month. Also speak of *ukuphala emasimi* (to scrape the gardens)

The great month for planting sorghum. Everyone very busy ploughing, sowing, weeding, building.

Intermittent storms. Stores low, hunger. Use of green vegetables and buying of grain. In bushveld mealies are nearly ripe. In the highveld still small. Month for locusts.

SUMMER (IHLOBO)

November *(Lweti):* A start, also a kind of insect of the same name, *Lweti,* which appears during this month. *Inkosi lencane:* Little King

Great agricultural activities. Weeding gardens. Some still planting beans. Building speeded up. Little *Incwala* (an agricultural ritual) may be held this month. Very late for planting mealies, but happens if rain was delayed.

Heavy rain in normal years. Nearing peak of hunger. Mealies ripening and some already ripe. Green caterpillars and grasshoppers, mushrooms and wild plants and insects. Brewing beer for 'little *Incwala*'. If mealies ripe, people eat them secretly, 'they steal', for permission has not yet been given. Taboo on pumpkin and mealie.

December *(Inkosi Lenkulu):* The big King: the big *Incwala* usually played in this moon. *Liduba* breeds in the bushveld, sometimes gives its name to the moon which is also known as *mavulangamiti, kuvungula,* to pick the teeth, *mita,* swallow

Weeding of gardens. Busy preparations for the big *Incwala.*

Peak of hunger before the big *Incwala,* hence the name *mavulangamiti,* to swallow the pickings of one's teeth. After big *Incwala* start on the new crops if they are ripe.

◁ **17** *Umngqusho*

This is the favourite dish in the Xhosa community, and various traditional bean types are combined.

Top left: Jugobeans
Top right: Cowpeas (type of bean)
Centre right: Mungbeans

Large mushrooms are gathered and fried on the embers.
   Many years ago the shells served as 'baby bottles' in the Xhosa society.

◁ **18 A variety of traditional dishes**

The ingredients used for these recipes have been part of African food culture for many years.

Dish in middle: Pumpkin and mealie meal. Xhosa: *Umqa wethanga/inqubela*; Sotho: *Setjetsa*; Zulu: *Isijingi*; Swazi: *Sidudvu*; Pedi: *Kgodu.*

Green dish directly above: Green sap paste. Xhosa: *Ingixi*; Sotho: *Motoho wa poone e ntjha*; Swazi: *Ligqotshelwa.*

Clockwise to the right, yellow squares: Fresh green mealies and pumpkin dumplings. Sotho dish: *Senyakama hiwana.*

Creamy crumble: Roasted groundnuts and roasted mealie meal. Tsonga dish: *Xigugu.*

Cereal mix: Mealie and sorghum stew.

Green-and-brown dish: Roasted groundnuts and green vegetables.

Chocolate-brown dish: Beans and sorghum meal. Sotho: *Sekgotho.*

White dish: Samp. Xhosa: *Ikeleko*; Sotho: *Setampo*; Venda: *Matutu.*

Light brown mix: Raw groundnuts, samp, beans and roasted groundnuts. Tsonga: *Tihove.*

◁ **19 Traditional dishes in modern guise**

Appetiser:
Fried pumpkin pips (served with traditional beer)

Main course:
Pheasant with marulas
Pumpkin and mealie rice balls
Venda porridge
Sorghum and groundnut dish
Cooked baby marrows

Dessert:
Fresh fruit (wild and cultivated)
Nuts (wild and cultivated)

This delicate Sotho dish, known as *dipolokwe,* is cooked in a 'traditional steamer' – a clay pot with reeds arranged criss-cross in the bottom. The pot is filled with water up to the reeds, the dumplings are spread over the reeds and steamed until done.

The dumplings are shaped into round balls by tossing them in a conical-shaped Sotho basket (*seroto*). When cooked, the dumplings are served in the same basket.

To kindle a fire for the cooking pots, either fire sticks or flint stones were used. The fire stick is rubbed between the hands with the point resting on a piece of soft wood. The friction creates the necessary sparks to set fire to pieces of dry grass. The same effect is achieved by hitting flint stones together.

Name of months of the year*

English name	Sotho name	Signification
September	Loetse	Pasturage – the grass springs up in the fields
October	Mpalana	Kind of iris which grows at this time
November	Pulunguana	Fawn of the gnu – this is the season when the female gnu produces her young
December	Tsitoe	Kind of cricket, which makes a good deal of noise at this time
January	Perekong	Coverer (moon of the) – the wheat begins to come into ear, and huts are erected for the shelter of those whose business it is to attend to the preservation of the products
February	Tlakola	Ear of corn
March	Tlakobela	Perfect grain
April	Mesa	To light – fires are now kindled, on account of the freshness of the mornings and evenings
May	Motseanong	Warbling of birds – it is cold, and the little birds warble through the valleys in search of food and shelter
June	Pupchane	Corn salad (a kind of)
July	Pupu	Name of the same plant, but without the termination *pchane*, which is a diminutive, because the plant is now found fully developed
August	Pato	Hidden – the pasturage of the last season is so dry that the cattle refuse to eat it; the fresh grass is still too short. The cows have no milk, or hide it, as the people say

*According to E. Casalis

Foods pertaining to
family events —

All feasts, whether the whole group participates or whether it is a family event, have a strong religious undertone. Traditional religious belief is in the ancestor cult – the belief in the immortality of the soul and the ancestor spirits guarding over their descendants. In all feasts and traditional ceremonies the ancestors are honoured and special offerings are made to the spirits. The place for the offerings varies according to the occasion as well as the group, the Nguni usually regarding the cattle byre or the grave of the ancestor as the holy place, while the Tsonga and Venda have shrines.

The offerings to the ancestors usually consist of beer, meal or other food or else the killing of an ox or bull or goat, and its apportionment according to fixed rules.

To cook the meat of the animals slaughtered for festivities, a 'sacred fire' is often prepared. This is done by starting a fresh fire: fire sticks are rubbed together till a spark is obtained to kindle a new fire. A hard piece of wood (called the male stick) is rubbed between the palms of the hands, while resting the point on a soft piece of wood (the female stick). The sparks thus developed kindle a fire in the dry grass arranged around the sticks. Twigs and larger pieces of wood are laid across the burning grass to prepare the flames for the large festive cooking pots. In tribes where a sacred fire is kept burning and is guarded all the time, a coal is fetched from there to start the fire for the festive cooking pots.

Rain-making ceremony

Rain is imperative to water the crops and in parts where low rainfall prevails regular ceremonies are conducted to 'entice' the much-needed rain. The rituals differ according to tradition and the professional rain maker can be the chief or a commoner. The Rain Queen, a mysterious lady living in a very special dwelling, is a cult of the Lobedu. Black animals like black oxen or goats are slaughtered during the proceedings and the cooked meat (as well as other food) is offered as sacrifice to the ancestors. An accompanying chant of *Pula, Pula* (i.e. 'Rain, Rain') is often heard amongst the Sotho people during these offerings.

traditional feasts and traditional taboos

In the Sotho society a rain-making ritual involving a porridge stick, is described by the Reverend S. S. Dornan. The porridge stick of the chief's wife is considered capable of drawing rain from the clouds and the women and girls would plan to steal this porridge stick. The womenfolk gather at the village, seize the porridge stick before the owner can prevent them and carry it off with joyful cries. The chief's wife pursues them to recapture the stick, but this is always unsuccessful as the precaution is taken to have the fleetest young women waiting at intervals along the way to carry the stick to the place of assembly. There the women sing their rain-making song, begging rain from a deceased chief who was a famous rain maker, Chief Solwane.

Solwane he, re batla pula	O Solwane! we want rain!
Helele! Pula e kae!	Oh, where is the rain?
Morena, re fe pula	Chief, give us rain
Re sala ka mehla re nyorilwe,	We remain always thirsty
Le likhomo li nyorilwe;	The cattle are thirsty;
Solwane, pula e kae!	Solwane, where is the rain?

Opening of agricultural seasons: hoeing, planting and harvesting

In many groups the chief formally opens each season of hoeing, planting or harvesting with a ceremony. The blessing and protection of the crops by the ancestral spirits are secured through these rituals and offerings to the ancestors are made in the form of food, usually beer or porridge.

The harvest or thanksgiving feast, referred to as the 'first fruits ceremony', is usually a very elaborate ritual. In the Swazi community this ceremony is sometimes called the 'killing of the bull'. This Swazi ceremony consists of two parts, namely the Little *incwala* and Great *incwala*. The first commences when the King, the central figure, goes into seclusion. On the second day of his seclusion, he is offered some concoction prepared by the medicine men and he ceremoniously spits it out.

The *incwala* dances are performed on the third and fourth days by maidens attired in their *incwala* finery and men, flamboyantly dressed in feathers, furs and beads follow suit with military dances.

The next day, a wild black bull is brought into the cattle kraal, provoked and then chased by naked youths, and is finally stabbed by the medicine man. The meat is ritually divided and eaten. Eventually the Queen mother, known as the 'she-elephant', arrives with a retinue of royal wives and they partake of the 'first fruits', thus signalling that the taboo on the eating of the ripening crops is lifted.

Throughout the activities large, festive cooking pots bubbling over fires to feed the crowds. Porridge and beer are served, but after the 'killing of the bull', meat and some of the delectable new crops like green mealies are added to the cooking pots.

Funerals

Deceased chiefs are honoured by the whole group and the funeral draws large crowds to the royal village. For this occasion, ritual slaughtering is done and in many societies the chief is buried in the skin of the black ox which is sacrificed for the funeral.

Meat, porridge, beans-and-mealies and vegetables are cooked in large cooking pots on open fires in the village and containers of beer are contributed by the visiting mourners. In the Venda community the fare is limited to unsalted sour porridge and meat to emphasise the forlorn atmosphere.

In the Pedi society, the meat served at a chief's funeral is referred to as *mogôga* and only initiated men are permitted to partake of it.

All funerals, also those of commoners, are habitually accompanied by the slaughtering of an animal and serving of cooked meat to the mourners. The Xhosa call this event *eyokukhapha,* i.e. accompanying the deceased to the ancestral world. In some communities it is the custom to slaughter a second animal after a year has elapsed and to serve food to 'put the spirit of the deceased to rest'. The Xhosa call this event *eyokubuyisa,* i.e. bringing the deceased home as an effective ancestral spirit.

Milk plays an important part in the 'purifying' procedures after a death has occurred. Milk calabashes are usually emptied and cleaned out, and milk is sprinkled over the object to be purified. It has been observed that lactating women enter the home of the deceased and squirt milk from their breasts around the house to purify it and make it fit for occupation. Sometimes bile from the animal slaughtered for the occasion is sprinkled around the house for purification purposes.

Marriage customs

Marriages are always looked upon as joyous occasions. The courtship and betrothal customs differ considerably among the different cultures, but all share the tradition of a gift of cattle to the bride's family. This gift is known as *lobola* amongst most people and acts as compensation for the loss of a daughter and her future children to the husband's clan.

Another feature common to all cultures is the extravagant marriage feast offered to the guests in-between traditional dances and customary games, such as stealing the bride. The favourite traditional dishes are served: meat and gravy, porridge, mealies, beans, and vegetables

Wedding guests

An African Thunderstorm

From the west
Clouds come hurrying with the wind
Turning
Sharply
Here and there
Like a plague of locusts
Whirling
Tossing up things on its tail
Like a madman chasing nothing.

Pregnant clouds
Ride stately on its back
Gathering to perch on hills
Like dark sinister wings;
The Wind whistles by
And trees bend to let it pass.

In the village
Screams of delighted children
Toss and turn
In the din of the whirling wind,
Women –
Babies clinging on their backs –
Dart about
In and out
Madly
The Wind whistles by
Whilst trees bend to let it pass.

David Rubadiri

Africana drawing of food preparation and

other rituals of an initiation ceremony

in season, such as pumpkin. Beer is offered as beverage and this traditional drink further enhances the happy mood. After a few days of festivities, the guests return home. The bride has usually already left with her new husband and the departing in-laws are supplied with food for the road. A hunk of cooked, salted beef and cooked cereal, and frequently left-over cooked mealies from the festivities, are taken along.

Until such time as the young wife is fully accepted in her new family, and this could well be until the first child is born or when her mother-in-law sees fit, she must observe a number of food restriction rules. The most prevalent taboo is that she may not drink milk obtained from her husband's cattle, as kinship is always indicated by the sharing of milk from the same herd. Once this ban is lifted, it is the sign that she can have her own hearth and cooking pots and display her own cooking skills.

The birth of a baby and names giving

These occasions are usually family affairs and different rituals are observed in the different communities. The birth of a baby is often marked with the slaughter of a goat. The meat is apportioned according to prescription between the family of the mother and father, and the soft skin is used as a blanket for the baby. In Xhosa this goat skin is called *imbeleko* and the goat *ibhokhwe yembeleko. (Ukubeleka* means to carry a baby on the back.) In the Venda society the meat is shared among the midwives and only at the names-giving ritual are the family invited to partake of beer, sour porridge and meat.

The naming of a baby is the prerogative of the father, and is not always accompanied by a family feast. Often a new name is bestowed at initiation ceremonies to signify that childhood is past.

Initiation

Teenage girls and boys are usually not accepted into the ranks of the adults until they have undergone initiation.

In most societies separate groups of girls and boys live in seclusion for a period ranging from a few days to a year (the latter in the Lobedu society). Special foods are served during this period of schooling the young in the traditions of the group and preparing them for adulthood and marriage. The foods are usually very simple and sparse, in keeping with the aura of 'hardship' in which the young are moulded. During this time the Xhosa boys are debarred from fresh or green foods, and are not allowed to feed themselves. According to Soga folklore, they have to be fed by their teacher. The dish containing the food must be placed at the boy's side, but if in front of him, it must be well away from his body or clothes to prevent him from contaminating the food. At this stage he does not eat facing forward, but turns his head to the side, and is spoonfed over his shoulder.

At the end of the period of seclusion the initiates are received back into the community with feasting and celebrations. Cattle or goats are slaughtered for the banquet and the people perform tribal songs and dances to the accompaniment of drums. The python dance of the Venda girls is particularly fascinating as they mimic the motion of a snake with the rhythmic sway of arms and body.

110

Python dance of Venda maidens at initiation ceremony

Other feasts

Other occasions that are celebrated by feasts and slaughtering of animals are the inauguration of a new chief, the reception of respected visitors, or in tribal societies that honour totems, the marriage of a boy and a girl who are related but who honour different totems. In this case, a sacrifice is made in order to counteract any harmful effects of the taboos placed upon marriage between related individuals.

Taboos

Some societies had totem animals believed to be house spirits of ancestors and it was taboo to eat these animals, although they may be sacrificed for ritual purposes.

The most common food taboo relates to milk consumption. Milk consumption indicates kinship and a man is prohibited from drinking milk in any household but his own or that of the paternal or maternal relatives. A woman may drink milk obtained only from her husband's herd and then only when she has been accepted into her new family. When she is considered impure, during menstruation or after a miscarriage, she has to avoid milk or working with milk containers.

Women and young girls are often not permitted to eat eggs lest they become infertile or acquire extra lovers.

Many groups impose food restrictions on pregnant women to the concern of nutritionists. Venda women must avoid vegetables, sweet foods and hot foods. During the last months of pregnancy she may eat very little, lest the baby grow too big and cause a difficult delivery. Pregnant women are usually barred from eating the flesh of an animal that died during giving birth, for fear that it might happen to them.

After birth, enormous amounts of thin porridge are served to the mother while most other foods are barred from the diet. This monotonous and insufficient diet is only relaxed once she is allowed to resume normal tasks. Before she may rejoin society she has to go through a purification ritual. The Zulu woman must springclean the hut and she is then sprinkled with purifying medicines. The Venda woman is formally visited by her husband in the hut and she must present him with a bracelet before he may accept food from her. Then she may prepare her favourite traditional dishes again.

Shona taboos

Do NOT eat kidneys; this might cause the death of your father or mother.

Do NOT eat the flesh or eggs of a nightjar; you might become habitually sleepy during the day.

Do NOT eat the flesh of a kingfisher; you might have bad luck.

Do NOT eat the flesh of an owl; it consorts with a witch and you may invoke the wrath of the witch.

A WOMAN must not eat the flesh of an animal's breast.

A HERD boy should not drink milk directly from the vessel in which it is left to settle; he may be drenched with rain whilst herding.

YOUNG PEOPLE should not eat the crop of a fowl; they may become forgetful.

Do NOT eat the flesh of a swallow as it does not eat grain.

YOUNG PEOPLE should not eat a fat mouse; they may lose their ability to procreate.

Do NOT eat the flesh of doves; you may develop epilepsy.

A PREGNANT woman should not eat the flesh of a grysbuck; her child may become constipated.

Do NOT eat birds' eggs; you may have fits of giddiness.

Do NOT eat small-winged flying termites; you may become deaf.

Do NOT eat a *bambara* nut that has been used in the game of spinning nuts; you may be attacked by dizziness.

Do NOT eat groundnuts dug up by a crow and buried again; you may become absentminded.

Do NOT eat maize grains that grow on the tassle; you may get boils or skin eruptions that prevent childbearing.

A MAN must not look into a stewpot; his eyes may become sunken and his face take on the shape of a baboon's.

Do NOT let one hand touch the ground while you are eating; you may one day suffer from starvation.

Do NOT lie down while you are eating; you may develop a stitch, pneumonia or a second navel.

A CHILD should not use a knife to put food in its mouth; its gums may shrivel.

Do NOT lie prone to drink from a well; you may catch an illness.

A SINGLE girl should never accept food from an unmarried man; there may be a love potion in it.

PART 2

SELECTED TRADITIONAL RECIPES

Names of crops

English	Botanical name	Zulu/ Swazi	Sotho/ Tswana	Pedi	Venda	Xhosa
Millet	Eleusine corocana; Pennisetum typhoideum	unyawothi	nyalothe/ lebelebele	pherefere		amazimba
Maize	Zea mays	umbila	poone/mmidi	mahea	mavhele	umbona
Sorghum	Sorghum spp.	amabele/ emabele	mabele	mabele	luvhele	amazimba
Melons	Citrullus spp.	beche	tjoto/ lehapu	morotse/ mogapu	mahabu	inty abontyi/ umxoxozi
Gourds	Lagenaria siceraria	liselwa/ iselwa/ amaselwa	seho/sego	moraka	zwitemba	uselwa
Cowpea	Vigna unguiculata	tindlubu/ tinhlumayo	dinawa	monawa	dzinawa	intlumayo
Jugobean	Voandzeia subterranea	tindlubu	dinawa	ditloo marapa		iindlubu/ iimboiyi
Mungbean	Vigna radiata	undonca	dinawa	dithlodi		
Groundnut	Arachis hypogaea	ematonga- mane	matokomane	dimake		amandongo- mane
Pumpkins	Cucurbita spp.	amathanga/ ithanga/ litsanga	mokopu/ lephutshe	mofidi	mafhuri	amathanga
Sweet cane	Sorghum brot	imfe	ntshwe/ mpshe	mpshe	movha/ mphe	imfe

Menu suggestions

To emulate African cooking, African taste and preference should be taken into consideration.

The favourite tastes are *bitter* and *sour-musty*. To obtain a bitter taste, gall is sprinkled over food, especially over fresh meat. When an animal is slaughtered, the contents of the stomach are often used to impart a bitter taste to porridge. Certain wild plants with a bitter taste are selected and added to the cooking pots.

MENU

SUMMER LUNCHEON/DINNER

Appetiser

Green sap paste	(p. 124)

Main course

Liver and meat	(p. 167)
Roasted mushrooms	(p. 157)
Mealie rice	(p. 129)
Cooked whole baby marrows	

Dessert

Fresh peaches and figs (instead of wild peaches and figs)

Beverage

Mahleu	(p. 177)

MENU

WINTER LUNCHEON/DINNER

Appetiser

Roasted pumpkin pips and roasted groundnuts

Main course

Stewed pigeon with gravy	(p. 168)
Bean and mealie stew	(p. 158)
Boiled pumpkin	(p. 155)
Stewed greens *(imifino/morogo)*	(p. 154)

Dessert

Stewed dried peaches (instead of dried wild peaches) served with honey
(Serving honey in the comb looks attractive and is authentic to African eating habits)

Beverage

Sorghum beer *(leting)*	(p. 173)

The following description of a recipe supplied by Enox Xotyeni illustrates the partiality to bitter foods:

Umgonyo

This was a favourite food of hunters. They would drain the water from the stomach contents of the antelope type of animals. The intestines were cut into small pieces and cooked with this watery stuff till well cooked. The sorghum powder or meal was then added. Gravy was added to make the food very loose. This had a very bitter taste but very tasty and nice when one was used to it. It was said to have great medicinal powers. The hunting dogs were also fed from it. The universal belief was that it was also immunising the hunters against snake bites. This was because the antelopes were immune to snake bites i.e. goats, duikers, bucks, springbucks, gemsbuck, blueduiker, and so forth.

The traditional sour-musty taste is obtained by fermenting cereals to use in sour porridges, beer and *amahewu*. These dishes are very prominent in the African culinary art. Sour milk, *amasi*, is often mixed with unfermented porridges and other cereal dishes to introduce a sour flavour to the foods.

MENU

OUTDOOR BARBECUE

First course

Steamed green mealie balls/dumplings   (p. 144)

Main course

Roast meat   (p. 167)
Thick mealie meal porridge   (p. 133)
Sauce made of greens *(imifino/morogo)*
   and roasted groundnuts   (p. 154)
Sweet potatoes baked in their jackets under
   the coals   (p. 157)

Dessert

Grapes and apples (instead of wild grapes and wild apples)

Beverage

Sorghum beer *(leting)*   (p. 173)

A food preference study done amongst the Swazi indicated that beer *(utshwala)* was ranked first. Meat was ranked second because it complements the sour taste of the beer, while the third was *phutu* (stiff porridge), but only when *amasi* (sour milk) has been added to it.

No condiments are used in traditional cooking, except salt. Most porridges are preferred without salt, but the side dishes such as gravy or pumpkin pips are heavily salted and are mixed *(shesheba)* with the porridge.

Salt was obtained in three ways in traditional society. It was gathered from areas where water had evaporated near the sea or other salt water sources. Salt was also extracted from alkaline soils by putting the soil in conical baskets and slowly pouring water through the soil. This solution was allowed to evaporate in the sun and yielded some coarse salt. A third source of salt was plants with a high salt content. The plants were burnt, the ashes washed and filtrated and the water evaporated through cooking to obtain the salt.

A *sweet* taste was appreciated in traditional society but a sweetening agent was never added to food. Honey was considered a snack and relished as such while sweet cane was chewed between meals.

The meal pattern consists of two meals during the day. Breakfast is eaten rather late in the morning and in earlier times consisted only of *amasi* (in the South Nguni societies). With the introduction of cultivated cereals, thin porridge became a very popular breakfast food and is usually served with sour milk.

The main meal of the day is served after dusk and consists of two dishes – a main cereal dish like stiff porridge or beans-and-mealies and a side dish in which the cereal is dipped. The side dish could be meat or meat gravy or vegetables like greens or pumpkin slices or any of the other traditional dishes. According to traditional belief this side dish eases the swallowing of the main dish. The main cereal dish can be made from one of a large variety of different cereals and thus can be mixed with other foods such as green leaves or fried melon pips or pumpkin or marula juice. A great number of these recipes are listed in the following pages.

Snacking between meals is common and *amahewu/mahleu*, a fermented cereal beverage, is consumed in great quantities to quench thirst and to still hunger pangs.

Traditional household containers were used for demonstration of recipes and measuring out of ingredients. It was necessary to convert 'a calabash scoop full' or 'a claypot full' to milligrams or millilitres. Recipes were not consistent and often varied according to the availability of ingredients. For this reason some recipes are given as 'one part of an ingredient to two parts of another ingredient'.

Salt, the only modern condiment used in traditional African cooking, was reserved for certain dishes only. The reader (and hopefully taster) may add salt if desired.

The field is vast and calls for interested persons from the many different cultural groups to record their particular ways of preparation of wild plants. Seasonal availability of plants and lack of preservation of these for markets remote from the source, exclude these ingredients for the purpose of this book. Recipes for a few of the most common of these dishes are however included.

The fascinating African cuisine warrants introduction to those unfamiliar with it. The menus are suggested for experimentation. Slight adaptations of these traditional recipes create exciting dishes with a distinct African flavour, as the menus above illustrate.

GOOD EATING!

Maize dishes

Green mealies

XHOSA: *Ibhaqolo ibangqa*
SOTHO: *Lephoto*
ZULU/SWAZI: *Infuto*
PEDI: *Lehlabula la lefela*
VENDA: *Mmopo o motola*

Ingredients Fresh green mealies on the cob
Salt (if desired)

Method Pick mealies when they are tender, but ripe. Remove the outer leaves, leaving the soft, green inner leaves that cover the seeds on the cob. Boil enough water to cover the mealies. Add a little salt to the water. Put the mealies into the boiling water and cook till tender, for approximately 30 minutes. Serve hot or cold.

Today a favourite way of serving piping hot green mealies is to spread butter on the kernels and eat them off the cob.

Roasted mealies

Ingredients Fresh green mealies
Salt (if desired)

Method Remove all the leaves from the cobs and roast the cobs on hot embers till the seeds are brown with a toasted aroma. Serve hot or cold.

It was traditionally served without salt and yellow maize was preferred for this dish.
Today it is a favourite at barbecues.

Dishes prepared from green mealies

The delectable flavour of fresh green mealies is pleasing to all palates, also those unfamiliar with African food.

Botanical name: *Zea mays*.

Maize, known as mealies in Africa, or in olden times as Indian or Turkish corn, is a more recent addition to the African diet than the indigenous cereals sorghum and millet. Yet the most favoured traditional dishes are prepared from mealies. It became part of the traditional cultural life, as the following Zulu proverb and Chinyanja riddle illustrate:

Zulu proverb: *Imbewu ihlalel' ihlanga layo* – the mealie seed waits for its stalk – meaning, the wrong will in due time propagate itself or have certain consequences.

Chinyanja riddle: *Kagomo kokwere ndi ana omwe* – a little hill which even the children can climb – indicating mealie meal porridge.

123

Green sap paste

XHOSA: *Inqixi*
SOTHO: *Motoho wa poone e ntjha*
SWAZI: *Ligqotshelwa*

Ingredients   Green mealie stalks
Fresh green mealies

Method   Pound a few young stalks, cover with water and boil until soft for approximately 1 hour. Strain off the fibrous material (this was traditionally done through a grass sieve). Reserve the liquid which has the aroma of fresh green mealies. Remove the mealie kernels from the cob and grind. (This was always done on the grinding stone.) Mix the liquid and the mealie seeds in the proportion of 1 part of liquid to 2 parts of ground mealies, e.g. 250 mℓ liquid to 500 mℓ ground mealies. Boil this mixture until cooked, approximately 20 minutes.

This dish with its delicate aroma was considered a delicacy in traditional African society and was also prepared from mealie stalks and tender, young sorghum ears.

For the modern palate, serve green sap paste as a delectable pâté, either hot or cold, e.g., as individual hors d'oeuvres, as a side dish with spicy meat, or spread on rye bread.

Cooked dry mealie seeds

XHOSA: *Inkobe*
SOTHO: *Likhobe/dikgobe*
SWAZI: *Tinkobe*
ZULU: *Izinkobe*
PEDI: *Lewala lefa lekokoro*

Ingredients   Dried ripe mealie kernels
Salt (if desired)

Method   Remove the dry seeds from the cob. Put the seeds into a cooking pot and cover with approximately four times the amount of water. Add salt if desired. Cook over very slow heat without stirring for approximately 5 hours, taking care not to break or mash the kernels. Add water if necessary.

The cooled dish is double the volume and weight of the kernels. The outer skin of the kernels rupture during cooking, and turn tender and mealy.

This dish with its nutty, sweet-salty taste was a traditional staple food. It used to be the dish that a hungry stranger, passing a village, would ask for.

This dish was regarded as a cleaner and beautifier of the teeth and was believed to give extra energy and strength. For the latter reason it was often carried on a journey or by hunting parties. It was known as *umphako* to the Xhosa.

The Zulu people today cook *izinkobe* with pieces of meat placed on top of the mealies to flavour the dish, which is then known as *umnyelankobe*.

Cooked dried mealies on the cob

Ingredients   Dried ripe mealie ears
Salt (if desired)
(After the ripe mealies have been harvested, some cobs are dried in their leaves.)

Method   To prepare a dish with a taste that is often likened to that of green mealies, remove the covering leaves. Cook the dried ears slowly for 2–3 hours in boiling water until the kernels are soft and swollen. Serve hot or cold, with or without salt, according to taste.
Serve these 'out of grean mealie season' at barbeques.

White mealies are preferred for this dish.

Ground dry mealie seed dishes

The innovative African woman extends the use of the dried mealie seeds by grinding them on the grindstone. Of this crumbly paste several dishes are prepared:

- *Umphothulo* (Xhosa); *mophothula* (Sotho); *umcaba* (Zulu): This dish is made by adding the crumbly paste to curds *(amasi/mafi)*. This soft textured dish has a nutty but tangy taste. In traditional society it was relished especially by the old and infirm. The custom was to put the crumbly paste in the *amasi/mafi* calabashes and eat it with a wooded spoon. No salt was served with this dish.

- *Umcuku* or *umbhantshi* was traditionally prepared by the Xhosa and Zulu. Soak the ground mealie paste in *amarehwu* (Xhosa) *amarewu* (Zulu) (a fermented cereal beverage). This dish has a sharp, tangy taste and is very refreshing in hot weather.

- *Incumbe* was an infant food prepared by the Zulu. The ground mealie paste was mixed with water, strained (traditionally through a grass sieve) and boiled.
  The nutritional value of *incumbe* was not sufficient to sustain growth and health in a child, but if the dish was served with milk and vegetables health and vitality were ensured.

- *Umcaba wemifino* is an interesting dish prepared by the Zulu. Press the ground mealie paste into flat pieces and place a layer of *imifino* (edible leaves of wild plants cooked like spinach) between the two layers of mealie paste, thus forming a sandwich.

- *Umbhuqwa*, a Zulu dish, is prepared by mixing mealie paste with ground roasted pumpkin pips. Roast the pumpkin pips in a pot till the outer hard coverings burst. Remove the inside seeds and grind. Mix equal quantities of mealie paste and ground pips. This dish has a pleasant, toasted, nutty taste. The mixture is often re-ground together on the grinding stone, as a delicacy for the connoisseurs of traditional African food.
  Umcaba as well as *umbhuqwa* can be included on vegetarian menus. Spinach can be substituted for *imifino*.

Toasted mealies

XHOSA: *Ugcado/incatsha*
SOTHO: *Sebera*
ZULU: *Utshewele*
SWAZI: *Imbasha*

Ingredients   Dried ripe mealie kernels

Method   The ripe mealie kernels can either be dry or soaked in water. Put the kernels into a cooking pot (it was traditionally toasted on a potsherd) and heat at a high temperature (this was always done over an open fire). Toast the seeds until they acquire a light brown colour – they might even swell and burst like popcorn, and have a similar taste. Serve hot.

This food was favoured at the morning meal, i.e. the first of the two daily meals.

Today this snack is very popular with cocktails.

Toasted mealies were also ground to a fine powder and shaped into balls. They were called *utshongo* (Xhosa); *dipabi* (Sotho); *lukhotse* (Swazi), and because they last long, were traditionally taken along on journeys or by hunting parties. A mouthful of toasted mealie powder, washed down with a drink of water, was cherished for its nutty flavour. It was also served with meat and gravy or with cooked green leaves of edible wild plants [*imifino* (Nguni); *morogo/moroho* (Sotho)].

Fermented whole mealie kernels

XHOSA: *Ihasa/irasa/isangcosi*

The seeds that cling to the sides of the storage grain pits tend to ferment. These were collected and ground and a fairly thin gruel or stiff porridge was prepared from it. Melon or pumpkin was sometimes added.

This dish has a strong flavour caused by the fermentation and is an acquired taste. It was popular at the time of the impis when it was used as a reserve food.

Samp

XHOSA: *Ikeleko*
SOTHO: *Setampo*
VENDA: *Matutu*

The practice of pounding mealie kernels in a wooden mortar with a wooden pestle, or sometimes with stone mortars and pestles is, according to anthropologists, of a comparatively recent origin. Grinding kernels between grinding stones was the original method of breaking up seeds for various traditional dishes, but pounding has become a favourite way to process grain. Among some Africans, samp cooked as a stew or mixed with beans or peas is preferred to porridges or whole cooked mealies.

During pounding the fibrous coating of the grain is broken and is then removed by winnowing.

Today samp is commercially processed by machine.

Ingredients	Samp
	Salt (if required)
Method	Wash the samp and add double the volume of water – e.g. 250 mℓ samp and 500 mℓ water. Soak overnight. Drain, add fresh water to cover and bring slowly to the boil. Simmer till soft, approximately 1½ hours, adding water when necessary. The cooked dish is double the volume and weight of the raw kernels. Salt can be added and a little fat, butter or margarine stirred into the mixture before serving.

It is served with meat dishes with a gravy, such as lamb stew, swiss steak, or meat balls and gravy.

Samp and beans is another very tasty combination and is listed under the legume dishes.

Mealie rice

As the name indicates, this is a new addition to traditional African food. The mealie kernels are broken down in the mortar to a size akin to that of rice grains, and then winnowed.

Machine-processed mealie rice is available commercially.

Ingredients	Mealie rice
	Salt (if desired)
Method	Cook and serve in the same way as samp. The cooked dish is double the volume and weight of the dry kernels.

Mealie rice is an interesting substitute for rice and combines well with curry stews, venison dishes, spicy beef or vegetarian bean sauces.

Mealie rice has also become part of a number of favoured traditional porridge recipes and these are listed under the porridges.

Porridges (gruels)

Porridge is the favourite food in the traditional Black cuisine of southern Africa.

The basic ingredient of porridges is ground grain. Although sorghum and millet are also used in porridge, the mealie is the most popular.

Mealie meal porridges

The grinding of the grain on the grinding stone is an arduous but specialised task, and this art is fast disappearing. In many societies the pounding block has replaced the grinding stone. A young girl was traditionally well versed in this household task of meal preparation. She was taught what the correct size of the particles should be for different dishes.

The fine nuances of traditional African cooking were probably best portrayed in the preparation of porridge, of which a great variety existed. For the best flavour, flour should be freshly ground, preferably just before the dish is prepared. Porridge made from a coarse grain has a taste and name different to that made of fine meal.

The African palate dislikes machine-ground maize flour. It is said that the machines impart a certain taste to the flour which is easily discernible. The grindstone releases the flavour of the maize and freshly ground grindstone flour is the food of the connoisseur.

To prepare porridge in the traditional way, the following utensils are needed:

- A clay cooking pot, relatively large mouthed to facilitate stirring.
- A meal basket/clay pot/calabash (for the freshly ground meal).
- A meal scoop (usually made from a small gourd with an elongated shape).
- A stirring stick/beater (a stick roughly 50 cm long with two thin sticks, approximately 10 cm in length, pushed at right angles through the point of the stick).
- A carved wooden spoon.

To cook a good porridge, the fire is important – neither too much nor too little flame. Traditionally two fire sticks were rubbed together to kindle the fire. The sparks would set fire to small twigs arranged around the fire sticks and when these were burning, two or three larger pieces of firewood were laid over the burning twigs. When these caught flame, they were arranged between the hearth stones, and the pot rested directly over the fire. Additional wood was added to keep a slow fire going.

To do justice to the porridge recipes, freshly ground grindstone flour should be used, but if not available, the commercial kinds could be substituted.

There are several kinds of porridges made from mealies. The most widely used recipes, and the mainstay of the African culinary art, are included.

Mukonde (Venda porridge)

To produce a runny porridge which sets quickly when cooled down, used to test whether a Venda girl had mastered the art of porridge cooking. The proportions are as follows:

1 part mealie meal (e.g. 250 mℓ)
2,5 parts boiling water (e.g. 625 mℓ)

For a dish of gourmet quality the mealie meal is freshly ground to an extremely fine powder and well winnowed to remove every particle of bran.

To prepare this special porridge, fresh water is put to the boil. One third of the flour is stirred into the boiling water by twisting the stirring stick briskly between the palms of the hands for approximately 2 minutes. Another third of the meal is added and the stirring continued for approximately 3 minutes. The remainder of the meal is folded in with the wooden spoon, followed by fast beating, and then stirred for a few minutes. This beating process is such that the porridge almost lifts out of the pot.

It is then left to cook over a slow fire for 15 to 20 minutes.

The finished product is a smooth, thick, viscous paste with a shiny, attractive pearly white colour and a pleasant nutty-sweet taste.

The Venda serve this porridge in a very specialised and fascinating way. The cooked porridge is ladled out in layers on a flat wooden dish. The process of ladling requires a special technique of spreading the porridge in thin layers, moving the hand outwards from the body. In this way an enlongated pyramid is constructed and usually three such structures are shaped on the large communal plate. On a smaller plate the layers are stacked in circular formation with a wide circle (like a pancake) at the bottom and a small circle (like a crumpet) on top.

This porridge is eaten in a prescribed way. Each person sharing the communal plate peels off one of these layers of porridge with the right hand and transfers it to the left hand. With the right hand, a piece is broken off, rolled with the fingers of the same hand into a ball and dipped into the side dish. As with all hand-eating techniques, etiquette demands that the fingers do not touch food in the side dish nor the mouth when the morsel is popped in.

The Venda have a special lidded basket which contained the plate with food of the father and he himself removed the lid and lifted out the plate.

Although this special porridge was called 'king's porridge', it was customary for the King or Chief of the Venda to have a male servant who was responsible for the preparation of his food. The skill of the women to dish out porridge in this special way was thus not necessarily developed in order to serve the food to the King, but rather to their husbands.

The serving procedure of other kinds of porridge was also prescribed by tradition. The man's portion was served from the centre of the pot. This was not only a token of respect but prevented malicious poisoning of the head of the house.

The man's porridge was often arranged in a dome shape and decorated with designs made by means of a mealie cob. The attractive geometric patterns displayed on the porridge indicated the wife's affection and it was often, in polygamous societies, a way to strive for favour from the husband. This decoration had an additional practical benefit in that it facilitated the formation of a skin over the cooling porridge which protected it from dust as well as drying out – dry porridge was considered unacceptable.

Thin mealie meal porridge

PEDI: *Bogobe bia bupi bia lefela motogo*
XHOSA: *Indengane/isidudu*
SOTHO: *Lesheleshele*
SWAZI: *Ledishela*
VENDA: *Metsi*
TSWANA: *Motoho*

Ingredients	Mealie meal
	Boiling water

The proportions of meal and water vary according to taste and custom, from 6 to 2,5 parts of water to 1 part of meal. By adding more water, a thinner porridge is obtained which is served mostly to nursing mothers, young children and invalids.

Method   Bring the water to the boil. Add the meal a little at a time and stir briskly (traditionally with a stick beater) to prevent lumps. Stir through (traditionally with a wooden spoon) and cook till done, about 20 minutes. The connoisseur, however, prefers the flavour that develops after simmering for 1–2 hours.

To prepare thin porridge in a modern kitchen, use a regular cooking pot (saucepan), beater, spoon and cooking appliances.

Traditionally thin porridge was served without salt, usually at the first meal of the day. To young children it was served with fresh milk and to adults with curds. A popular way to serve thin soft porridge today is with sugar and fresh milk as a breakfast food.

Thick mealie meal porridge

XHOSA: *Iphalish/isishwala/umqa*
SOTHO: *Bohobe*
SWAZI: *Sishwala*
TSWANA: *Shokwana*

This was the favourite food at the evening meal. It is still preferred by people doing hard manual work as it 'lasts long in the stomach', a traditional expression.

Ingredients
2 parts mealie meal (e.g. 500 mℓ)
1 part boiling water (e.g. 250 mℓ)

Method
Bring fresh water to the boil in a pot. Add all the meal directly to the boiling water. Leave to cook for approximately 10 minutes, then stir the mixture thoroughly, and cook slowly for 30 minutes. Stir again and serve.

Another way of cooking this porridge is to stir one quarter of the meal into the boiling water to form a big lump and let it simmer for 5 minutes. Then add the remaining meal and stir until all the lumps have disappeared. Cook for 30 minutes more over slow heat.

A third method is to make a paste of the meal with a little cold water. The paste is stirred into the boiling water and cooked for 20 to 30 minutes over a slow heat and then served.

Today thick porridge is served with sausage and gravy, with tomato-and-onion sauce or as a side dish to the family meal.

Crumbly mealie meal porridge

XHOSA: *Umphokoqo*
ZULU: *Puthu*
SWAZI: *Uputhu*

Ingredients
4 parts mealie meal (e.g. 1 ℓ)
1 to 2 parts boiling water (e.g. 250/500 mℓ)

Method
Boil fresh water and pour the meal in all at once, but do not stir. Place the lid on and allow the water to bubble through the meal. Stir the mixture and reduce the heat. Cook over low heat without stirring until it is done, about 20 minutes. The connoisseur simmers this porridge for an hour or two to improve the flavour.

This porridge is the favourite of the Zulu people. It is served with *amasi* (sour milk) or vegetables or with a gravy made from beans or meat.

Crumbly porridge is very popular today at outdoor meals, served with barbecued meat and spicy sauces. With bean gravy, it is a very tasty and nutritious vegetarian dish.

Other porridges

Both millet and sorghum are indigenous to Africa and early in the history of African man became part of his diet. These two cereals are thus basic to African dishes and although maize replaced it as the most important cereal in traditional cooking, dishes made from millet and sorghum are still relished as delicacies.

Many traditional proverbs and ritual practices reflect the interwovenness of these cereals with everyday life. When a Pedi says, 'How can a man refuse to help his mother's brother who has given him *ubwali* [millet meal porridge]?', he indicates the importance of kinship obligations. In traditional ritual festivities, finger millet beer was the favourite and the Venda would serve it at the harvest festival or present it as a special gift to the headman.

Millet meal porridges

Botanial names of plants used:

Eleusine corocana
Pennisetum typhoideum

Thick millet meal porridge

PEDI: *Bogobe bjabupi bja leotsa*
VENDA: *Bogobe jwa lebelebele*
ZULU: *Igqiza*

As with maize porridge, meal freshly ground on the grindstone yields the best results.

Ingredients	1 part millet meal (e.g. 250 mℓ) 2 parts water (e.g. 500 mℓ)
Method	Boil the water in the cooking pot. Add one third of the meal and stir briskly. Cook for 3 minutes. Add another third of the meal, stir in briskly and cook for 2 minutes. Fold in the remaining meal and stir well. Cook over a slow heat for 10 minutes.

This dish has a delicate taste with a musty, bitter-sweet flavour. The texture is thick and viscous and it has an attractive light-brown colour.

Traditionally this dish was served with a relish like wild spinach (*imifino/moroho*) or a salty delicacy like mopani worms, or sour milk (*amasi/mafi*).

135

Thin millet meal porridge

PEDI: *Motepa wa bupi bja leotsa*
ZULU: *Tncimbi/umncindo*
XHOSA: *Isidudu*
TSWANA: *Motogo wa lebelebele*

Thin millet porridge was traditionally served as a breakfast food or as a food for children, in the latter case with fresh milk.

Ingredients   1 part millet meal (e.g. 250 mℓ)
              2 parts water (e.g. 500 mℓ)

Method   Boil enough water to cover the stirring stick or beater. Add the meal slowly in small quantities and stir vigorously with the stick to prevent lumping. Cook over slow heat till all the meal is absorbed and cooked, approximately 15 minutes.

These tasty, attractive millet porridges would brighten any modern winter breakfast table, but unfortunately millet is no longer readily available.

Sorghum meal porridges

Botanical name:
Sorghum spp.

Thin and thick sorghum porridges

Both thick and thin porridges were traditionally prepared from sorghum meal. The same proportions of meal and water and the same preparation procedure as for millet porridge were used.

These porridges differ from millet porridges in that thick sorghum porridge has an attractive reddish-brown colour and an appetising, nutty-sweet taste. The thick porridge is called *bogobebja bupi bja mabelethoro* by the Pedi; *iyambazi* by the Zulu; *umqa wa mazimba* by the Xhosa and *ting ya mebele* by the Tswana.

The thin sorghum porridge, the *motepa wa bupi bja mabelethoro* of the Pedi and the *motogo wa mabele* of the Tswana, was traditionally served with fresh milk to children and nursing mothers. It is served with sour milk *(amasi/mafi)* as a breakfast food for adults.

On contemporary breakfast tables the malted sorghum porridges are not only attractive, but pleasant tasting as well.

A very thin sorghum porridge made from finely ground sorghum grain as food for infants is called *incumbe* by the Zulu and *inembe* by the Swazi.

Mealies, a later addition to the cooking pots, are combined with the older, traditional cereal sorghum to produce favourite dishes.

136

SWAZI: *Iyambazi*
TSWANA: *Mmatshule*

Thin sorghum and mealie rice porridge

Ingredients   1 part sorghum meal (e.g. 100 mℓ)
1,3 parts mealie rice (e.g. 130 mℓ)
8 parts water (e.g. 800 mℓ)

Method   Soak the mealie rice overnight in 2 parts of water (e.g. 200 mℓ). Mix the sorghum meal and 2 parts of water (e.g. 200 mℓ) to a soft paste. Put the rest of the water to boil, add the mealie rice, and cook for 5 minutes. Stir the sorghum meal into the mealie rice and cook for 20 to 25 minutes, stirring occasionally.

The porridge was traditionally served either hot or cold as a substantial breakfast dish.

Thick sorghum and mealie rice porridge

Ingredients   1,5 parts sorghum meal (e.g. 150 mℓ)
1 part mealie rice (e.g. 100 mℓ)
6 parts water (e.g. 600 mℓ)

Method   Follow the instructions as for thin mealie rice porridge, but take care to stir the sorghum meal paste in small quantities into the boiling mealie rice, stirring all the time, and cook for 20 to 25 minutes.

This dish was traditionally sought after as an accompaniment to a salty relish.

Sweet milk porridge

XHOSA/SWAZI: *Isidudu*
SOTHO: *Lehala*
PEDI: *Legala*

A very tasty dish of gourmet standard is prepared from fresh milk and ground green mealies.

As a substitute for green mealies, ground, dry mealie meal or freshly ground sorghum meal may be used.

Ingredients	1 part ground fresh mealies/dried mealies/sorghum (e.g. 250 ml) 6 parts fresh sweet milk (e.g. 1,5 ℓ) Salt (if desired)
Method	Heat milk to boiling point. Add salt. Sprinkle ground cereal on top and stir slowly to prevent the formation of lumps. Simmer till the porridge is cooked, for approximately 15 to 20 minutes.

This dish has a smooth creamy texture and the colour varies depending on the cereal. Made from green mealies, the porridge has a pale, creamy-green colour and prepared from sorghum a light, creamy-brown colour is obtained.

On the modern menu, the green mealie porridge and milk can be served as a very appetising soup 'with a difference'.

Baobab milk porridge

The fruit of this majestic African tree is considered a delicacy. The acid flesh is pounded in the pounding block and mixed with milk for a delectable, thick porridge.

Ingredients	1 part baobab flour 2 parts fresh milk
Method	Stir the flour in the milk. When the acid in the flour has thickened the milk, it is ready to serve.

Sour milk or whey porridge

Some Africans, like the Pedi, use sour milk to cook their *mpshi*, but others like the South Sotho use the whey to prepare their *motoho oa lloea*.

Ingredients   1 part meal (sorghum/millet/mealie)
                 3 parts either sour milk or whey

Method   Follow the directions as for sweet milk porridge.

The dish has an agreeable tangy-sweet taste and the colour depends on the ingredients used. Sorghum imparts a rich strawberry-brown colour to the dish and the mealie an opalescent white colour.

   These sour milk porridges were very popular in traditional society. They were usually served as a cold, thick porridge and eaten with the fingers.

Colostrum porridge

XHOSA: *Umthubi/isithubi*
ZULU: *Isithubi*
TSWANA: *Bogobe jwa kgatsela*

Ingredients   The thick yellow milk of a cow after she has delivered a calf (colostrum), called *umthubi* by the Xhosa
                 Meal, either mealie or sorghum

Method   Immediately after milking, put the colostrum in a pot and heat slowly. Stir until thickened, but do not boil. When the milk stops coagulating add enough meal to produce a soft porridge.

This dish was traditionally eaten by young herd boys who may have invited other herd boys to share it with them. Girls who had not yet reached puberty were not permitted to eat of this porridge.

Fermented porridges

These porridges are greatly relished by the Africans but is an acquired taste for the uninitiated. However, once one has grown accustomed to the dish, it could well become a great favourite.

The South African peoples traditionally prepared their own special fermented porridges or, as it is popularly known, sour porridges.

These fermented porridges, with their sour-musty, slightly bitter taste are still a favourite dish of many Black people as well as of people from other cultures who have acquired this taste.

Thin sour porridge

The *ting* porridges of the Sotho are prepared from sorghum, millet or mealie meal and water. The proportions differ but the preparation procedures are similar.

Ingredients — Sorghum (1 part sorghum, 3 parts water)
Millet meal (1 part millet meal, 3 parts water)
Mealie meal (1 part mealie meal, 4 parts water)

Method — Heat the water till lukewarm and stir it into the meal. Leave for 24 hours to ferment, then decant the water and put to the boil. Ladle the sediment into the boiling water and stir briskly with the stirring stick. Beat thoroughly with a wooden spoon and cook over a slow heat for 15 to 20 minutes. Serve either hot or cold.

The *incoho* of the Xhosa and the *motoho* of the Sotho is a thin, sour porridge.

Ingredients — 1 part mealie meal (e.g. 250 mℓ)
1 part lukewarm water (e.g. 250 mℓ)
3 parts cold water (e.g. 750 mℓ)

Method — Mix the meal and lukewarm water and leave to ferment for 24 hours in a closed container. Boil the rest of the water, stir in the fermented mealie meal and cook for approximately 15 minutes. Serve with or without sugar.

Thick sour porridge

Ingredients
1 part fermented mealie meal (as prepared for thin sour porridge) (e.g. 250 mℓ)
2 parts mealie meal (e.g. 500 mℓ)
4 parts water (e.g. 1 ℓ)

Method
Boil the water, add the fermented mixture and stir briskly. Stir in the mealie meal, taking care that no lumps are formed. Cook over low heat for approximately 15 minutes. Serve hot or cold.

• *Umcuku:* The Xhosa people traditionally prepared *umcuku*, which was only fermented after cooking was completed. The procedure was to prepare *umphothulo* (ground cooked mealies) or *umkhupha* (mealie meal bread) or *sishwala* (stiff porridge). This was then crumbled and mixed with *amarehwu* (fermented cereal used as beverage) to a stiff paste and left for further fermentation, until it was served.

• *Seqhaqhabola:* The Sotho people prepared *seqhaqhabola* in the following way: Mealies were ground coarsely between grinding stones, moistened and left for 6 hours. This paste was ground again and four times the quantity of very hot water was poured on and left to cool. A small amount of leftover sour porridge was stirred into the mixture (often called 'yeast') and left for a further 12 hours. The water was decanted and boiled and the sediment stirred briskly into the boiling water with a stirring stick. It was left to cook for approximately 15 minutes over a slow fire and served hot or cold.

• *Isibhebe:* The Zulu prepared *isibhebe* by grinding sprouting sorghum seeds. A thin mealie meal porridge was prepared and cooled off, the sorghum malt added and the mixture put aside to ferment for 12 to 24 hours. It was then served cold as a thin porridge.

Mealie rice and mealie meal sour porridge

Ingredients
1 part mealie rice (e.g. 125 mℓ)
2 parts mealie meal (e.g. 250 mℓ)
4 parts water (e.g. 500 mℓ)

Method
Mix the mealie meal (250 mℓ) and 2 parts lukewarm water (250 mℓ) and leave to ferment for 24 hours. Boil the rest of the water, add the mealie rice and cook for 5 minutes. Add the mealie meal and gently mix the ingredients with a stirring stick. Cook slowly for 25 minutes, stirring occasionally until the thick mixture is cooked. Serve either hot or cold.

Beer sour porridge

SWAZI: *Insekese*

Ingredients
The leftover dregs in the beer brewing pot
Porridge, either thin or thick, made from mealie meal, a mixture of mealie meal and mealie rice, or sorghum meal

Method
Strain the dregs in the beer brewing pot (traditionally this is done by means of a grass sieve). Add this liquid to the prepared porridge and leave to ferment for a few hours.

The Zulu people often made this porridge called *unxuku* or *umbantshi* in the evening and left it overnight to ferment. It was served cold as a breakfast food the following morning.

Sweet cane, also known as sweet reed *(sorghum saccharatum; sorghum brot)*, is indigenous to Africa. The stem of the plant has a sweet juice and is chewed as a snack.

To prepare a gourmet dish from sweet cane, tender young green mealies are crushed on the grindstone and boiled in the sweet cane water to yield a sweet, tasty porridge.

The sweet juice used in porridge water is extracted in the following way:

Bruise the cane stalks and put them into a cooking pot (saucepan) containing a small quantity of water, enough to cover the stalks. Boil for approximately 15 minutes and cool. Squeeze the stalks to release all juice and add to the remaining liquid in the pot.

Strain and use as liquid for a thick porridge of mealie meal or sorghum meal.

Parboiled porridges

This was a special and tasty dish prepared in some African societies. Sorghum, whole mealies or samp was parboiled to facilitate grinding of the seeds. After grinding, it was mixed with sour milk *(amasi/mafi)* to produce a paste and served at the evening meal. If eaten at breakfast, it was believed to cause dullness and fatigue.

These porridges were traditionally prepared by most Blacks in southern Africa. Variations of the basic recipes were developed in certain areas, for example in areas where marula trees grew, marula juice was used instead of water in preparation of the porridge and it imparted an almost apricot-like flavour to the porridge. Other wild fruits were used in the same way, thus creating a variety of recipes.

Porridges mixed with vegetables were also prepared according to traditional tribal tastes. Examples are the *isidudu* of the Swazi, a thin pumpkin-and-maize-melonseed porridge.

The total number of different porridges prepared by the various peoples in southern Africa could well be more than 70.

Dumplings

A variety of dumplings were prepared in traditional African cookery. Of all the African dishes, dumplings seemed most familiar to early White travellers and mention is made in old documents of 'cakes' or 'breads' eaten in traditional society.

Dumplings were not a regular dish but were served by way of a change, instead of porridge. They remain fresh and moist for several days and were thus admirably suited as food for travellers.

Dumplings were prepared from mealie meal, sorghum meal or millet meal. To prepare tasty mealie meal for this dish, hard, ripe mealie seeds were ground coarsely, and hot water was sprinkled over the mealies. After soaking for two hours, the mealies were ground again – this meal was called *intlama* by the Xhosa.

To cook dumplings the batter was either dropped into boiling water, or steamed in a pot on top of boiling meat or in a traditional steamer.

The latter was cleverly constructed by placing sticks, mealie cobs or grain stalks in a crisscross fashion in a clay cooking pot. The pot was filled with water up to the level of the sticks and the dumplings were placed on top of the sticks. The water was brought to a boil and replenished when necessary. Mealie or pumpkin leaves were sometimes wrapped around the dumplings.

Mealie meal dumplings

Steamed green mealie balls/dumplings

ZULU: *Isinkwa sombila/ujeqe*
SOTHO: *Dipolokwe*
XHOSA: *Isigezenga*
TSWANA: *Mantebelekwane*

Ingredients	Fresh green mealies Salt (if desired) Mealie or pumpkin leaves
Method	Remove the fresh mealie kernels from the cob and grind. (This was traditionally done on a grinding stone.) Add a little salt and mould the paste into balls. (These can be flattened and shaped as desired.) Wrap these balls in mealie or pumpkin leaves or wax paper and steam in a perforated steamer for approximately 1 hour, or until done.

Traditionally these wrapped mealie balls were steamed in the clay pot with crisscross-sticks steamer.

This dish was usually served like bread, or broken up and eaten with sour milk. The latter is known as *amasi* to the Nguni people and as *mafi* to most Sotho groups.

144

The Sotho people varied the mealie ball/dumpling recipe by adding mashed pumpkin to the green mealies. This gave an attractive yellow colour to the dish, which was called *senyakama hlwana*.

The delicious aroma and taste of the steamed fresh mealies and the interesting way of wrapping these balls will intrigue guests at brunches, luncheons or barbecues.

A modern adaptation of this recipe reads as follows:

Ingredients	5 medium-sized mealie cobs (remove the leaves and the kernels) 125 mℓ bread flour 12,5 mℓ baking powder 12,5 mℓ salt Mealie leaves
Method	Grind the fresh mealie kernels until fine. Add flour, baking powder and salt, making a soft dough. Put the fresh leaves of the mealies in a crisscross fashion in the bottom of a deep saucepan with water, put the dough on top, cover the dough with leaves and steam till done, approximately 30 minutes.

Steamed mealie meal dumplings

ZULU: *Fusazana*

Ingredients	1 part mealie meal (e.g. 250 mℓ) Water, about two thirds the amount of mealie meal (e.g. 160 mℓ) Salt to taste
Method	Fill a pot one third with water, place sticks crisscross over the water and bring to a boil, or use a perforated steamer. Mix the meal, water and salt into a dough. Form the dough into a ball and wrap it in mealie leaves. Steam for approximately 2 hours. Cut into slices and serve. (This is a very tasty accompaniment to meat at a brunch or barbecue.)

The likeness of dumplings to bread has resulted in two Xhosa names for dumplings, namely *isinka sombona* (bread made from mealies), and *isinka samanzi* (bread made from water).

In traditional Xhosa cooking, a cup of beer, *igweli*, was mixed with the meal and water in the preparation of dumplings. The fermentation process leavened the dumplings and imparted a sourish taste.

Boiled mealie meal dumplings

SOTHO: *Maqebenkwane/bohobe*
XHOSA: *Umkhupha/udodroyi*
PEDI: *Dinkgwa tsa bupi bja lefela*

Ingredients
1 part mealie meal (e.g. 250 mℓ)
Water, about two thirds the amount of the mealie meal (e.g. 160 mℓ)
Salt to taste (the older the meal the more salt is added)

Method
Mix the mealie meal, water and salt into a dough. Shape into large, round flat cakes, 50 mm thick and 150 mm in diameter – square shapes were also made. Bring the water to a boil in a pot and place the flattened dumplings along the inner sides of the pot. Boil for approximately 2 hours, replenishing the boiling water when necessary.

An alternative method is to form the dough into a ball and wrap it in mealie leaves. Place the dough on top of sticks or cobs and steam for approximately 2 hours. Cut into slices and serve.

A very soft dumpling is prepared by leaving the meal and water mixture for a few hours until the meal is fully hydrated.

Dumplings were traditionally served with a side dish of meat gravy or vegetables. The Sotho cooled the dumplings and served them with milk.

These dumplings add interest to a meal when served instead of potatoes with a stew such as beef curry or venison. It can also be cut into slices and served at a brunch or barbeque.

146

Meat mealie meal dumplings

Ingredients
1 part mealie meal (e.g. 250 mℓ)
1,5 parts water (e.g. 375 mℓ)
Salt to taste

Method
When the boiling meat is almost cooked, mix the mealie meal, water and salt into a soft batter. Dish spoonfuls of batter onto the boiling meat and let them steam for approximately half an hour, or until cooked. Serve the dumplings with the meat.

The hot dumplings are scooped out of the pot with a spoon, but the experienced cook lifts the dumplings from the pot with her fingers. Scalding is prevented by dipping the hand in cold water after every dumpling has been removed.

These dumplings 'extend' the meat dish for a large family. It is very tasty when served with spicy beef, lamb or pheasant stew.

Sorghum meal dumplings

These dumplings have a reddish-brown colour and a pleasant nutty, sweet taste, not unlike wholewheat bread.

Ingredients
1 part sorghum meal (e.g. 250 mℓ)
3 parts water (e.g. 750 mℓ)
Salt to taste

Method
Mix the ingredients into a dough. Shape the dumplings and cook either by steaming in a steamer or placed on top of meat or by boiling in water (see mealie meal dumplings). Sorghum dumplings can be served as a breakfast cereal on a cold winter morning.

Dumplings made from unripened sorghum

This is a speciality of the Sotho people who call it *senkgwana sa mabele*.

Ingredients   Unripe sorghum
                       Water

Method   The sorghum is threshed before the grains have hardened and ground to a pulp on the grinding stone. Enough water is mixed with the pulp to prepare a soft dough.

A steamer is prepared by putting a small amount of water in a clay pot and putting reeds crisscross above the water.

The pot is put to the boil and the batter poured on top of the sticks and steamed for 2 hours, the water being replenished when necessary. The reed sticks are removed and the sorghum in the pot is stirred to a pulp for approximately 30 minutes. While still hot, some of the pulp is placed in a conical-shaped basket called a *seroto*, and rolled to form a ball. The balls are rolled round and round in the basket to acquire a smooth surface.

The ritual of preparation and shaping of these dumplings is intriguing and could provide much fun at a brunch.

Ingredients   1 part millet meal (e.g. 250 mℓ)
                       1,5 parts water (e.g. 375 mℓ)
                       Salt to taste

Method   Mix the ingredients into a soft dough and mold by hand into balls. Bring a pot of water to the boil and drop the dumplings into the water, allowing the bottom layer 2 minutes to set before the next layer is added. Steam over slow heat for 40 minutes.

Simple cereal dishes

Fine millet seeds were used for traditional dishes eaten raw. The Zulu prepared the following two dishes:

- *Umlaba/igiza:* The small millet grains were crushed on a stone to break away the husks, which could easily be blown away by mouth. This cleaned grain was then sprinkled with water and ground into a very fine paste. It was served as a snack.

- *Iyambazi/incimbi:* This dish differs from the previous only in that the crushed grain was mixed with more water, to form a thin uncooked porridge which was eaten as breakfast food.

When the ears were fully developed but still milky, they were picked for a special dish. To prevent scorching, a layer of sorghum leaves were put in the bottom of the pot and the sorghum ears laid on top, covered with water and boiled slowly for approximately 40 minutes. When unripe mealie ears were cooked, a few outer leaves were left to protect the cobs.

The cooked ears were allowed to cool in the pot and were served from the pot.

The sorghum kernels were stripped off by drawing the spikelet through the teeth; the mealie kernels were rubbed from the cob and tossed into the mouth.

Both dishes were traditionally served as a snack to people who were hoeing or planting in the fields.

Ingredients	1 part whole dry sorghum seeds (e.g. 250 mℓ)
	3 parts water (e.g. 750 mℓ)
	Salt to taste
	or
	1 part whole dry mealie seeds (e.g. 250 mℓ)
	3 parts water (e.g. 1 ℓ)
	Salt to taste
Method	Both cereals are simmered over a slow fire until soft – for approximately 2 to 3 hours.

Both dishes were traditionally served as a staple food, usually at the main meal of the day.

Vegetarians may serve these stews with a bean dish to create a nutritionally balanced protein meal.

Mealie and sorghum stew

Ingredients	1 part whole dry mealie seeds
	1 part whole dry sorghum seeds
	6 parts water
	Salt to taste
Method	Simmer over a slow fire for 2–3 hours.

It is a very tasty dish for outdoor cooking and is an excellent accompaniment for sausages and gravy.

Cooked cereal with sour milk

VENDA: *Legala*

Ingredients	Any suitable mealie or sorghum dish
	Enough sour milk *(amasi/mafi)* to serve it with

- *Inkobe* (cooked dried mealies) and *amasi*.
- *Umphothulo* (cooked sorghum, ground afterwards) and *amasi*.

Once the taste is acquired the cereal and curds is a favourite dish of people not of the African culture. The dish is likened to muesli and yogurt.

Cereal and vegetable mixes

The ingenuity of the Black woman has resulted in a variety of dishes using a few basic ingredients, for example cereals and vegetables.

Pumpkin and mealie meal

XHOSA: *Umqa wethanga/ingubela*
SOTHA: *Setjetsa*
ZULU: *Isijingi*
SWAZI: *Sidvudvu*
PEDI: *Kgodu*

A large variety of pumpkins are grown in southern Africa and any of these can be used for this dish. The traditional procedure of preparing a pumpkin was to cut it open and peel it by scraping with a spoon (a knife was not to be used). The seeds were removed and kept for another traditional dish.

Ingredients
1 medium pumpkin
250 mℓ mealie meal
Salt to taste

Method
Boil the prepared pumpkin in salted water until almost tender. Pour the mealie meal on top and steam for approximately 15 to 20 minutes, adding water if necessary. Stir the mixture well to produce a stiff porridge.

This dish was often prepared during the winter months, from pumpkins stored for several months. Melons (*umxoxozi* in Xhosa) with white flesh, could be substituted for the pumpkin.
  (This recipe was sometimes prepared with sorghum meal instead of mealie meal.)

Pumpkin and mealie rice

Ingredients   1 medium pumpkin
125–250 mℓ cooked mealie rice
250 mℓ mealie meal

Method   Prepare the pumpkin as for pumpkin and mealie meal. When almost cooked, add the cooked mealie rice and stir. Pour the mealie meal on top and steam for 20–30 minutes. Stir through. Serve with fresh milk.

Pumpkin and green mealies

XHOSA: *Umxhaxha*
SOTHO: *Senyakamahlwana*

Ingredients   5 parts pumpkin (500 g peeled)
2 parts green mealies (200 g cut from the cob)
5 mℓ salt

Method   Prepare pumpkin as for pumpkin and mealie meal. Boil in salted water until almost cooked. Put the green mealies on top and cook for approximately 15 minutes. Mix and serve.

The *mahlwana* (eyes) in the Sotho name indicate that the mealies resemble staring eyes.

Melon, roasted melon seeds and mealie meal

PEDI: *Sempjerane*

Ingredients
1 medium melon
500 mℓ mealie meal
100 g roasted and ground melon seeds
Salt to taste

Method
The melon is prepared in the same way as described for pumpkin and mealie meal. Traditionally the dried seeds are prepared by roasting them on a potsherd and grinding them to a fine powder on a grindstone.
Boil the melon in enough water to cover until almost tender. Pour the mealie meal on top and steam for 10 minutes. Add the ground seed and salt and stir well. Cook for a further 10–15 minutes. Serve hot or cold.

This dish can also be prepared with sorghum meal instead of mealie meal. Sometimes a little mealie rice is added for variation.

Greens and mealie meal

ZULU: *Isiqwamba*
XHOSA: *Isigibane/umqubela/umfino*
SOTHO: *Potele*

A large variety of wild greens are collected and can be used for this dish.

Ingredients
A basketful of greens (e.g. 2 ℓ)
One or two mugs of maize meal, enough for the amount of green leaves (i.e. 250–500 mℓ)
Salt to taste

Method
Wash the leaves thoroughly and cut into strips. Bring enough water to a boil to cover the leaves. Cook the leaves for a few minutes. Add the maize meal and steam for 15–20 minutes, adding water if necessary. Mix well to produce a thick porridge.

Vegetable dishes

Imifino *(Nguni)*; morogo/moroho *(Sotho)*

The wild greens gathered on tilled lands, in the veld, and on hillocks next to water sources vary in different parts of the country. In each area the Black people know which leaves, pods, tendrils or flowers can be made into a vegetable stew.

According to Dr P. J. Quinn who researched the food habits of the Pedi people, 'Gathering vegetative material for pot-herbs is no haphazard function; to the contrary, the desired portions are selected carefully and nipped off with the finger nails. Even greater care is exercised when material is collected from cultivated plants so as to avoid damage to the growth of the plant and thus impair its primary function.'

Called *imifino* by the Nguni and *morogo* or *moroho* by the Sotho, this dish is part of all traditional southern African food cultures. The different species of plants might impart a different flavour to the dish, but the recipe remains basically the same.

Ingredients: Any edible wild or cultivated leaves, pods, tendrils or flowers suitable for stewing (spinach could be used instead), salt to taste.

Method: Sort and wash the plant material. Boil a little water in a cooking pot and add the plant material. Boil until tender and add salt. Serve with porridge or on its own.

Imifino serves as an *isishebo* (mixing agent) for *uputhu* porridge in the Zulu society and is a very popular dish.

In some societies, older boys and men regarded this as food to be eaten only by womenfolk. However, after a drinking spree this food was eagerly consumed by all who suffered from the after-effects of too much alcohol.

The dish is still very popular in modern society, but adaptations have been made by adding onions, tomatoes, potatoes and sometimes chillies.

Pumpkin tendrils

XHOSA: *Imitwane*
VENDA: *Morogo wa mofodi/phutshe*
SOTHO: *Lepu*

This stew is made from the delicate terminals of pumpkin runners. If not enough of those, some pumpkin flowers or soft leaves might be added.

This dish has a delicate taste and is still considered a treat.

Dried greens

The leaves were dried during the summer months and kept for winter when veld food was not available. Pumpkin leaves and bean leaves, as well as those from edible wild plants, were preserved by boiling them in water, squeezing out the water and shaping them into patties. These were spread on stones and dried in the sun.

The dried leaves have a dark green, almost black colour and have lost much of its piquant taste. A better method of preserving these leaves is to only dry it in the sun, thus preserving the taste of the leaves.

The dried leaves were cooked in the same way as the fresh *imifino* or *morogo*.

Monawa (dried bean leaves) and *lerotho* (dried edible wild leaves) were relished by the Sotho people.

The *imifino (morogo)* is sometimes cooked in milk instead of water.

Setjetsa (a Sotho dish)

Ingredients   1 part dried leaves
                1 part pumpkin pieces
                1 part mealie meal

Method   Cook the leaves for approximately 20 minutes. Add pumpkin and meal and cook for a further 30 minutes. Stir, add salt if desired, and serve.

Pumpkin

XHOSA: *Ithanga*
SOTHO: *Mokopu*

These huge, brightly coloured vegetables are attractive and eye-catching at modern African agricultural shows. Huge melons and calabashes add to the display, although the latter are only used in *imifino (morogo)* dishes when the plants are very young.

Hard-shelled pumpkins are called *usenza* by the Xhosa. The boiled pumpkin is known as *inqeke* to the Zulu and *amaceba* or *inxotha* to the Xhosa.

The hard-shelled pumpkins grown in other parts of the world can be used with success in these recipes.

Boiled pumpkin

The traditional way to prepare a hard-shelled pumpkin was to cut it in large slices, scoop out the inside with a spoon and simply cook them in boiling water with the peel on, until soft. The slices were served whole.

Sekele is a Sotho dish made by peeling the pumpkin, boiling it until soft and stirring it to a pulp before serving it with salt.

Pumpkin mixes

Pumpkin with bright yellow flesh, called *ithanga* by the Xhosa, is cut into smaller pieces, peeled with a spoon and boiled until almost soft. A quantity of dough, consisting of dampened mealies, mealie meal or beans, is added and cooked for a further period until everything is cooked. It is then mixed, and served.

(For recipes see under cereal and vegetable mixes.)

These same dishes were prepared by using melon.

Dried pumpkin

XHOSA: *Ugwadugwadu/uqwaqwadu*

To preserve pumpkin or melon for the winter it was cut into pieces and dried on the thatch of the roof. When required it was soaked in water and cooked in the same way as the fresh product.

Roasted pumpkin or melon seeds

SOTHO: *Dithotse*

Roasted seeds were usually not served alone, but were a tasty accompaniment to cereal porridges. The seeds were eaten one at a time, and relished with a lump of porridge.

Ingredients   10 parts whole, dry pumpkin or melon seeds (e.g. 500 g)
1 part salt (e.g. 50 g)

Method   Wash the seeds in water to remove the waxy outer layer. Put an empty dry pot or pan on the fire and heat well. Add the wet seeds, sprinkle with salt and stir continuously. Heat until the seeds crack – approximately 5 minutes.

This very appetising dish is served either hot or cold and is an interesting snack with cocktails.

Giant mushrooms are collected by the Xhosa as a great delicacy and a favourite food during the summer months. It is eaten raw with salt, roasted on coals, or fried in fat in a frying pan or on a potsherd. Salt is added before the fried mushrooms are served.

Sweet potato

The sweet potato is of relatively recent introduction to the African diet but is a popular vegetable. It is prepared either by boiling it in water or roasting on coals without peeling. It is served instead of porridge, quite often as *isishebo* for meat.

Amadumbe

This potato-like vegetable is, contrary to popular belief, not indigenous to Africa, yet it is so well liked by most Zulu people that it is cultivated despite the fact that it takes 7–11 months to ripen.

The amadumbes are prepared by boiling them in water until done, peeling off the skin and sprinkling with salt before being served.

Ilaxa (mixed vegetables)

A stew similar to *imfino (morogo)* is prepared by combining the leaves of spinach, cabbage and turnips. Oil or fat may be added to the dish.

Legume dishes

Beans

In addition to the two bean varieties indigenous to Africa, i.e. jugo-bean and cowpea (which is a bean), many other varieties have been incorporated in traditional cooking. The high protein content enhances the nutritive value of the diet. Any kind of dried beans can be used for the following recipes.

Bean and mealie stew

XHOSA: *Idubay*
MPONDO: *Uphethwana*
SOTHO: *Umqhafuneyko*

This dish was especially popular with the Xhosa people and was considered to be their staple dish rather than porridge. This dish was traditionally prepared for festivities like weddings or harvest festivals.

Mealies, green or dry, are boiled together with beans. The proportions differ according to the occasion: beans usually constitute one third of the dish, but may be less or more.

Ingredients

2 parts mealies (e.g. 500 mℓ)
1 part beans (e.g. 250 mℓ)
Salt to taste (e.g. 10 mℓ)

Method

Wash the mealies and beans and soak overnight in enough water to cover. Boil fresh water to cover (± 1,5 ℓ) and add the drained beans and mealies. Cook for approximately 3 hours, replenishing water when necessary to obtain a soft (but not watery) consistency. When well cooked, add salt and stir. Serve with meat gravy and a vegetable.

Samp and bean stew

XHOSA: *Umngqusho*

Follow the same recipe as for beans and mealie stew, but use samp instead of whole mealies.

Modern recipe for *umngqusho*

Ingredients
125 g beans, soaked overnight
125 g samp, soaked overnight
500 g brisket, cut into cubes
1 onion, chopped
2 tomatoes, chopped
1 green pepper, chopped
Salt, pepper, lemon juice to taste

Method
Cook the beans and samp as for *umngqusho*. Brown meat and onion, add salt, pepper and water to cover and simmer until almost done. Add onion, tomato and green pepper and simmer till the ingredients are cooked. Mix with the *umngqusho*, add lemon juice to taste, heat through and serve.

Variation of *umngqusho* recipe

Substitute one quarter of the beans with roasted peanuts. Grind the peanuts and add to the cooked dish shortly before it is served.

Isopu/umqhavunyeke (Xhosa)

Mealies and beans were often served to large crowds, such as at a funeral or a harvest festival. To ensure that sufficient mealie and bean stew was available at serving time, the amount of water was increased and the cooking time extended to 6 hours. A dish with the consistency of soup was obtained and this was usually served over porridge.

Bean and sorghum stew

XHOSA: *Uphethwana/inyakavu*
SOTHO: *Sekgotho*

Ingredients   3 parts beans (e.g. 750 mℓ)
1 part sorghum (e.g. 250 mℓ)
Salt to taste (e.g. 10 mℓ)

Method   Soak the beans overnight, drain and cook in fresh water till almost soft. Add the sorghum and more water and cook until the mixture is soft and all the water is absorbed. Stir well and serve.

This dish has a very satisfying sweet-nutty taste.
Inyakavu can also be prepared from fresh, ripe, shelled beans, in which case soaking is unnecessary.

Beans and sorghum meal

SOTHO: *Sekgotho*

Ingredients   3 parts beans (whole dry) (e.g. 750 mℓ)
2 parts sorghum meal (e.g. 500 mℓ)
Salt to taste

Method   Soak the beans overnight, drain and cook in fresh water until soft. Mash and add salt. One third of the sorghum flour is stirred in and cooked for 2 minutes, another third is stirred in and cooked for 2 minutes and the last third is stirred in thoroughly and cooked for 10 minutes.

This light brown coarse mash has an appetising flavour and was traditionally served with a vegetable side dish.
It can be served in the same way to people of other cultures.

Stewed bean relish

PEDI: *Lewa*

Bean relishes were served as a side dish with stiff porridge. Lumps of porridge were broken off with the fingers and dipped into the relish.

Ingredients   Any kind of dried beans
Salt

Method   Put the beans in a cooking pot and cover with water. Stew over a slow fire for 2–3 hours, stirring occasionally, but avoid breaking the kernels. The salt is stirred in when the beans are cooked.

Bean gravy

PEDI: *Setopja*
VENDA: *More wa nawa*

This dish is prepared from crushed beans and is served as a side dish with porridge.

Ingredients   1 part dried beans, any kind (e.g. 250 mℓ)
5 parts water (e.g. 1,25 ℓ)
Salt to taste

Method   Beans are crushed coarsely on the grinding stone and winnowed. The water is brought to the boil in a clay pot and the crushed beans gradually stirred in. This is cooked for approximately 40 minutes, the consistency being that of soup, and served either hot or cold.

This dish makes an excellent soup on a winter dinner menu.

Groundnuts (peanuts)

This legume is a later addition to the traditional diet, but with its pleasing, rich taste was soon incorporated into traditional recipes.

Roasted groundnuts

The seeds are roasted in the pods on hot coals, shelled and eaten. The raw shelled nuts are roasted on a potsherd over the fire. It is relished today as a snack with drinks.

Roasted groundnuts and green vegetables

When leafy green vegetables, i.e. *imifino* or *morogo* is almost cooked, a handful of ground, roasted groundnuts is stirred in and cooked for a further 5 minutes.

The appealing taste of this dish has induced modern cooks to add a spoonful of peanut butter to leafy green vegetables before serving.

Roasted groundnuts and mealies

Ingredients	2 parts roasted, shelled groundnuts (e.g. 500 mℓ) 1 part whole mealies or samp (e.g. 250 mℓ) Salt to taste (e.g. 10 mℓ)
Method	Boil the mealies for approximately 1 hour. Add the groundnuts and cook till tender. Add the salt and let it simmer for 15 minutes. Serve hot or cold.

Raw groundnuts, samp, beans and roasted groundnuts

TSONGA: *Tihove*

Ingredients
2 parts samp (e.g. 500 mℓ)
1 part beans (e.g. 250 mℓ)
1 part raw groundnuts (e.g. 250 mℓ)
1 part ground, roasted groundnuts (e.g. 250 mℓ)
Salt to taste

Method
Soak the samp and beans overnight. Drain and boil in fresh water for approximately 1 hour. Add the raw groundnuts and boil until everything is soft. Stir in the roasted groundnuts and mix well. Add the salt, simmer for 15 minutes and serve.

An interesting vegetable dish for the modern table.

Roasted groundnuts and green mealies (roasted on coals)

VENDA: *Mukhomo*

Ingredients
2 parts green mealies, removed from the cob after it was roasted (e.g. 500 mℓ)
1 part roasted groundnuts (e.g. 250 mℓ)

Method
Stamp the mealies and groundnuts together and mix. It will have the consistency of fudge. Serve as an appetising first course on the modern menu. It can be cut into squares and served on a small plate.

Roasted groundnuts and roasted mealie meal

TSONGA: *Xigugu*

Ingredients

2 parts roasted peanuts (e.g. 500 mℓ)
1 part roasted mealie meal (e.g. 250 mℓ)
Salt (e.g. 10 mℓ)

Method

Pound the peanuts in a mortar until they are fine and a compact mass. Add the roasted mealie meal and salt and grind until the mixture has a coarse texture and creamy colour. Serve as a paste with porridge. (This paste was often compacted in a calabash container and kept very well for a couple of weeks.)

Meat, including wild birds, rodents and insects

Although meat was enjoyed by the traditional community, cattle and goats were not slaughtered simply to obtain food.

Meat was served to the guests at festive occasions such as weddings, initiation ceremonies, births and even funerals. At such occasions all the meat was eaten during the festivities and it was not necessary to preserve meats.

If, however, an animal was killed by accident or died through natural causes, the meat was preserved by cutting it into thin strips and drying it for later consumption. The Swazi call this dried meat *umcweba*.

The meat supply was sometimes supplemented through the success of a hunting party, but the hunters all received their share of the quarry and this left a scanty supply for the individual cooking pot.

The traditional method of cooking meat was very simple: the meat was either roasted on the embers, broiled on a stick skewer over the flames, or boiled in water. Salt was the only spice added to the meat.

More important than the cooking procedure, was the division of the carcass. The procedure was not the same in all societies and the following is a description (according to Jones) of the ritual among the Swazi people:

The ox is usually slaughtered in the early afternoon when the men of the neighbourhood foregather at the home of the host, but women are forbidden to visit. The male visitor is expected to consume his portion before departing, but he is permitted to carry a small portion home 'for the dogs' (i.e. his children).

The animal is slaughtered with a spear and then skinned, the first bite of the flesh is taken by the head of the house or the guest of honour, or both. The male visitors can then consume the 'stolen portions' *(amantshontsho)* which they have removed during the skinning. The carcass is hung in a hut and the ragged portions or trimmings given to the women. The latter also receive the 'insides', except the spleen, liver, heart and sweetbreads *(amalulu)*. Women prior to menopause are forbidden to eat that part of the entrails known as *umsasane*.

Early the following day the men roast and eat the forequarters *(umkono)*, while the women are apportioned the ribs. The contents of the facial sinuses *(bopondveni)* are removed, and these, together with the sweetbreads and a certain liver lobe *(umphundvu)* are roasted for the grey-haired men, and the senior old women. It is to be noted that the elderly, who are held in much respect in Black society, receive the soft, easily chewed portions.

The top vertebrae *(sankala)* of the beast are taken as a present to the local chief by a youth or young girl. The remainder of the meat is boiled in large pots. The herdboys take from the pot their prerogatives, the upper lip *(ingcova)*, the appendix *(umntshaza)* and a certain portion of the stomach *(tsandlwane)*.

While the meat is cooking, the *bubende* is being prepared. The ingredients are small pieces of fat from the peritoneum, the lung tissue, blood and salt. These are boiled together and the resultant thick mixture is eaten while the stomach is comparatively empty.

The boiled meat is distributed, the women having the hind leg *(umlente)* and some of the ribs, the men the remainder; but the brisket *(umganga)* is left in the pot, or put on one side. The fat part of the gravy is skimmed off into a clay pot.

The men eat near the cattle kraal, but the women partake in the privacy of the huts. As the evening comes the visitors depart, while the immediate family *(lusenduo)* gather outside the reed screen of the big hut *(indlunkulu)* to eat the brisket *(umganga)* and to discuss family affairs.

On the third day, the hooves *(amasondvo)* are cooked. If a guest is departing the haunch may be boiled in salted water, and then salt rubbed in *(umkhunsu)*. Eaten cold, this will provision a journey lasting several days. It is on the third day the *sidlwadlwa* is eaten; to the reserved fat portion of the gravy is added finely ground sorghum preferably, or maize meal. The dish is given to important guests and adults, it is considered too rich for children.

Very fat gravy mixed with ground sorghum or maize or as a side dish to any kind of porridge or cereal, is relished by tribal people. The low fat content of the regular diet explains this preference.

Traditional meat dishes are not very well known, but a few are described below:

Matlala

Among the Sotho people this dish was served to middle-aged and old women. Small pieces of all parts of the carcass of an ox or a cow, i.e. neck, rump, rib, tongue, liver, heart, stomach etc., were cut off and chopped up very finely. The mixture was stewed for 7 to 8 hours and flavoured with salt.

It was served as a side dish with thick porridge, but young women, men and children were not allowed to partake of it.

Bubende/ubende

This dish was prepared by the Nguni people. Blood and small pieces of fat were cooked together. The *bobete* of the Sotho was almost similar, when the blood, stomach and intestines of a goat were combined. The *bobêtê* of the Pedi is made from the same parts but cut from a bullock carcass.

The blood of the slaughtered goat was collected and allowed to coagulate. The clotted blood was kneaded and the fluid discarded.

The stomach and intestines were boiled for 3–4 hours and cut up into small pieces and returned to the pot. An equal amount of blood was added and stirred over the fire for 20 minutes, after which salt was added. It was then ready to be served.

This dish was forbidden to young women who had not yet had a child.

Lekgotlwane

This is a dish of minced meat prepared by the Sotho. Goat meat was boiled for 8–10 hours, the fat strained off and all the bone and sinew removed. The meat was then pounded in a wooden pestle till finely shredded. It was then returned to the pot, cooked for 10 minutes, salted and served.

This dish was especially popular at wedding banquets.

Roast meat

Meat roasted on the embers or on spits was the favourite meat dish of men and was the only food the menfolk prepared. The meat was always underdone, being only scorched on the outside. It was commonly eaten while drinking sorghum beer.

In the Swazi community strips of meat as well as kidneys, liver and entrails are prepared on spits.

Boiled meat

The whole cut of meat is placed in the pot and boiled. In the Zulu society dumplings, especially mealie meal dumplings, were frequently steamed on top of the meat.

This large piece of meat was then placed on a wooden dish, cut into small pieces and eaten with the dumplings (msheba).

Dried meat

Meat is preserved by either cutting it into strips and drying it in the sun (called umcwayiba in the Swazi community) or the meat is cooked with certain plant material for preservation. In Venda, stamped seeds of the rulonga and marula are mixed with the cooked meat to preserve it. The Swazi's call their preserved cooked meat umkhunsu.

Xiridza

This is a Shangaan dish prepared from dried meat, which was cooked in water until tender, and a handful of ground, roasted peanuts stirred in. After adding salt, it was served.

Liver

Liver was relished in most societies and roasting over the coals was a favourite way to prepare it. It was customary to prepare the liver soon after slaughtering, often while the carcass was still being divided.

The appetising aroma of the liver on the coals encouraged everybody to work faster on the division of the carcass and get down to the enjoyment of cooked meat.

In modern times, liver roasted over coals enhances outdoor cooking specialities.

Liver and meat

Liver was sometimes cut up and mixed with finely cut meat from the rest of the carcass. The chitterling (vetderm) of the animal stuffed with this mixture and fried over coals, was a very tasty dish.

This dish can be likened to the well-known chitterling sausage and could be an interesting delicacy at any barbeque today.

Game

The meat of larger game was prepared in more or less the same way as that of cattle. However, venison was often served cold to diminish the strong odour of cooked game.

Wild birds

In traditional society no chickens or other domesticated birds were raised. However, wild birds were in abundance and were quite often hunted for the pot. Traps were set for guinea fowl, partridges and doves. Other birds like wild peacocks, cranes, bustards and even plovers were usually hunted by throwing a club at them. Numerous other birds were also eaten, as long as they were not considered a totem symbol of the particular society.

The most common way in which wild birds were cooked, was to truss them, stew them slowly till soft, and serve them with gravy. Sometimes meat was stirred into the gravy until it became a fine pulp and was served with stiff porridge.

The trussed birds were also roasted over coals, much like the modern chicken barbeque. This was the way the herd boys prepared the wild birds they hunted during the day while the cattle or goats were grazing in the veld.

In some societies the untrussed birds were covered with clay and baked under glowing coals or in a hole in the ground with a fire or glowing coals spread over the hole. When the clay was removed, the feathers of the bird came off with the clay and left the juicy tender flesh as a delectable dish.

Rodents

The vlei rat feeds on cereals and plant material and this rodent as well as the smaller field mouse were tasty titbits in some traditional societies. They were usually prepared by the herd boys. The innards were removed, the small animals laid on the smouldering coals to roast and the skin pulled off after it was cooked.

In the Shona society the vlei rat was called *chirwaneneso* and in the Nguni society field mice were called *imbiba* and rats *libuti*.

In the Zulu society the herd boys chased the field mice out of their holes by dancing and hutting the ground with sticks, while they sang:

Woza mbiba woza o'mankolo wami (come fieldmouse, come).

Insects

Large numbers are often collected during the night after a swarm has settled.

Locusts

Tinjiya (Tswana recipe)

Remove the wings and hindlegs of the locusts, and boil in a little water until soft. Add salt (if desired) and a little fat and fry until brown. Serve with cooked, dried mealies.

Sikonyane (Swazi recipe)

Prepare embers and roast the whole locust on the embers. Remove head, wings and legs – in other words only the breast part is eaten.

The South Sotho people used locusts especially as a food for travellers. The heads and last joint of the hindlegs were broken off and the rest laid on the coals to roast. The roasted locusts were ground on a grinding stone to a fine powder. This powder could be kept for long periods of time and was taken along on a journey.

Dried locusts were also prepared for the winter months in some traditional societies. The legs, when dried, were especially relished for their pleasant taste.

Different kinds of ants are collected as food, depending on occurence.

Ants

Majenje (a Tswana recipe for red ants)

The ants are obtained from an anthill. Boil the ants until they die. Add salt and fat, and fry until roasted.

Tintshwa (a Tswana recipe for flying ants (black as well as white))

The ants are obtained from an anthill. Boil the ants in a little water. Remove the wings. Add salt and fat and fry until brown.

Tinklwa (a Swazi recipe for white flying ants)

The flying ants are collected, the wings removed and the ants fried in their own body fat in a clay pot. It has a pleasant taste like crackling and is served as a snack or as a side dish with porridge.

Pupae

An anthill is opened up and the fat white pupae removed. These are put into a clay pot and fried until brown.

Different caterpillars are eaten in different societies, depending on location. The method of preparation is usually to squeeze out the insides, wash them and either fry them in their own body fat in a cooking pot until they are brown, or cook them in a little water.

Caterpillars

The caterpillars are often dried to preserve them throughout the year. They are cleaned, boiled and then spread out in the sun to dry. To cook these, they are first boiled in a small amount of water and then fried in fat.

The best-known caterpillars are those feeding on the mopani tree. They are called *masonja* and are relished by the Northern Sotho people.

The Venda eat the *mashonza mufhulu* caterpillar, similar to the mopani caterpillar and prepared and cooked in the same way.

Modern recipe for dried *masonja* (mopani worms)

Ingredients	250 mℓ dried mopani worms
	5 mℓ salt
	25 mℓ oil
	1 onion
	1 tomato
Method	Soak the mopani worms in hot salted water until they have swollen out and drain the water off. Boil them in a small amount of fresh water and drain. Fry in oil, adding chopped onion and tomato. Simmer until tomatoes and onion are cooked and serve hot with porridge.

Sand crickets

These appear in the summer months and were regarded as a delicacy in some traditional societies.

The crickets are collected, their wings and forelegs removed, the intestinal contents squeezed out and the rest grilled in a clay pot. They are stirred until brown, salt added and served with porridge.

Beetles

Many different kinds of beetles feeding on trees or grass are collected in different areas.

The most common method of preparation is to remove the legs and wings and squeeze out the innards. The beetles are then washed and grilled in a clay pot until they are crisp. Salt is usually added before the dish is served.

milk

Milk was a favourite foodstuff in all traditional southern African cultures although its use was prescribed by numerous taboos and rituals.

Milk was usually preferred sour and only the very young or the old and infirm partook of fresh milk.

The milk sacks used in the very olden days have given way to other containers and the Xhosa and Zulu later used calabashes to prepare their *amasi*, but the South Sotho people preferred a clay pot for their *mafi* and the Pedi used either a clay pot or a calabash in which to prepare *sanya*.

The calabashes usually had a hole in the bottom with a stopper, and the usual way to prepare curds was to draw off the whey at the bottom and to add fresh milk at the top. It was regularly churned with a stirring stick, or else the calabashes were shaken until the curds were ready to be served. A little was left in the container to start the fermentation process of the following batch of milk.

Thick curds were usually served on their own or as a side dish with porridge or with ground cooked mealies.

Fresh milk was traditionally served only to small children but was more often used in the preparation of milk porridges.

The whey – called *intloya* by the Xhosa – was often drunk as a beverage, especially by children or women working the fields.

The cream was often skimmed off the milk and churned – not to be used as food, but as a cosmetic for the skin called *sereledi* by the South Sotho.

Other beverages

Apart from water and milk, the other beverages included in the traditional diet were beer (made from grain), palm wine, ciders made from various fruits and a fermented honey drink.

Beer was by far the most important beverage and was universally made. It was not merely considered a beverage, but was consumed as a food. Furthermore, the important role of beer in social and religious ceremonies elevated it to a higher status than that of a mere beverage.

Light beer

XHOSA: *Amarehwu*
ZULU: *Amahewu*
SWAZI: *Emahewu*
PEDI: *Metogo*
SOTHO: *Mahleu*
VENDA: *Maphulo*

This beer is made from mealies and is non-intoxicating. It resembles a thin fermented porridge and is drunk any time of the day to quench thirst and to provide nourishment until the next meal is served.

Ingredients — Mealie meal or freshly ground crushed mealies
Small amount of malted sorghum ground into a paste

Method — Prepare a thin porridge from the mealie meal or ground mealies and cool down. Add the sorghum paste and leave in a warm place till it froths (approximately 1 day). Serve without straining.

Leting – A mild Sotho beer

Ingredients   1 kg germinated sorghum meal
                      3 ℓ water, lukewarm
                      250 mℓ of a previous *leting* brew

Method   The sorghum malt is pre-prepared by sprouting the sorghum seeds, drying them and grinding them on a grinding stone to a meal flour.

                      Put the meal in a pot, add a litre of boiling water and stir for 5 minutes. Cool to room temperature. Add 2 ℓ of water and 250 mℓ of leftover *leting*. Leave for 18 hours in a warm place. Stir again, strain (traditionally this was done through a grass sieve) and serve.

Strong (intoxicating) beer

ZULU, SWAZI: *Utywala*
XHOSA: *Utywala*
SOUTH SOTHO: *Joala*
PEDI: *Bjalwa*
TSWANA: *Bogale*
VENDA: *Mela*

Although numerous recipes were used in traditional societies, these beverages are all made from malted cereal, either from sorghum, millet or maize (mealies) or from a mixture of these.

Usually malted sorghum was preferred for the 'yeast' and either of the three cereals used for the 'body' of the mixture.

Beer-making was a specialist craft held in high esteem by traditional society as all religious ceremonies and other festivities featured the presentation of beer or the drinking of beer as part of the ritual. In everyday life beer enhanced social 'visits' and contributed to the nutritional value of the daily menu.

The following Pedi recipe for malting sorghum is the general procedure in most societies for producing 'strong' beer.

Malting

Traditionally the Pedi used only sorghum and millet for malting, but nowadays mealies are also used. The process of malting sorghum which is similar for all cereals is described as follows by Quinn:

Method

1st day: Whole, dry, clean grain is placed in a clay pot (*moeta*), and sufficient cold water added to submerge the grain completely. The container is stood in a cosy spot.

2nd day: After 24 hours the grain has commenced to sprout. The grain is drained and transferred to a grass basket (*seroto)*, and stood in a cosy spot.

3rd day: After 24 hours plumules have reached a length of 6 mm. The sprouting grain generates heat which makes it an attractive lair for the family cat, and since the Pedi know that pressure reduces rate of sprouting, the cat is watched carefully.

4th day: Sprouting allowed to continue without interference.

5th day: Plumules have reached a length of about 25 mm and the sprouted grain has become an entangled mass. This is dumped on the earth floor of the hut-enclosure (*lapa*), broken up and allowed to dry in the sun. When sufficiently dry the grain is ground into coarse meal on a grinding stone.

Beer prepared from sorghum, malt and mealie meal

Ingredients

1 part white mealie meal (e.g. 1 kg)
4 parts sorghum malt (e.g. 4 kg)
16 parts water (e.g. 16 ℓ)

Method

1st day: Mealie meal (750 g), sorghum malt (1 kg) and boiling water (4 ℓ) are stirred together in a clay pot (*moeta*). The pot is closed and stood in a warm place for approximately 40 minutes. Additional amounts of mealie meal (250 g), malt (1 kg) and cold water (8 ℓ) are added to the pot, and the contents stirred through. The container is closed and stored for 24 hours in a warm spot.

2nd day: Sorghum malt (1 kg) and boiling water (2 ℓ) are stirred in a separate clay pot and left in a warm place for approximately 30 minutes. This liquid is decanted into a cooking pot, water (2 ℓ) is added and brought to the boil. The contents of the two pots are mixed and cooked for 1 hour. The brew is then transferred to a storage pot and stored for 24 hours.

3rd day: The contents of the pot have formed a thick gelatinous mass. Sufficient dry malt (1 kg) is added to liquify the mass. The contents are stirred thoroughly and the pot stored in a cosy place.

4th day: The product is screened. If 'strong' enough, it is strained through a basketry strainer into a clay pot, ready to be served.

If it is not 'strong' enough the fermentation continues for another day.

Beer made from wild fruits (sometimes called 'wine' or 'cider')

Numerous wild fruits are gathered for intoxicating drinks and even wild melons are used in some societies.

The most popular and strongest drink is made from the marula fruit. These trees grow in the northern regions of southern Africa and ripen during the hot summer months. The etiquette for drinking, which allows any passerby to dip into the beverage pot, makes the marula season one of the most convivial of the year.

Method

Peel off the outer layer (traditionally this was done by picking it off with a sharpened stick), and remove the pips. Extract the juice from the pulp by pressing it between the hands. Then add water (approximately double the quantity of juice) and pour into a clay pot or beer basket. Cover the container and leave to ferment in a warm spot for a day or two (traditionally the pot was covered with pumpkin leaves). When foam has formed on top the beverage is ready for consumption. Strain off the foam (traditionally this was done through a grass sieve) and serve.

Wild honey beer

According to old records, fermented honey was used in the Xhosa societies before sorghum beer was introduced. This intoxicating beverage of ancient origin was made by extracting the dark brown honey made by wild bees in hollow trunks or crevices in rocks from the honey comb. A few larvae left in the honey enhanced the fermentation process.

Water was mixed into the honey and the container was left for a few days to ferment, thus producing an extremely potent drink.

Ilala /milala palm beer

Near the coast, this palm grows wild. In the traditional society each palm was 'owned' by somebody in the neighbourhood and these rules of possession were strictly adhered to.

The method to obtain the juice from this plant was to cut a slant in the top shoot (or growing point) of the palm. A juice exuded from this slit and a container was held underneath to receive the juice.

This juice was transferred to a clay pot and left to ferment for a few days. The owner of the palm tree thus had his own 'beer plant' for his household needs.

Modern recipes for beer

These are made with industrially prepared malt or yeast which cut down on the preparation time.

Ingredients	700 g mealie meal (coarse)
	5 ℓ water
	25,0 g malt starter (available commercially)
	10 mℓ dried yeast or 1 or 2 cubes compressed yeast

Method	Mix the mealie meal into the water and boil for 1 hour. Cool until it can be touched, and stir in the malt starter. Cool to body temperature. Add the yeast and ferment for 24 hours. Strain through a muslin cloth and serve.

Modern recipe for *amarehwu/amahewu/mahleu*

Ingredients   625 g mealie meal
                          5 ℓ water
                          50–100 g ground whole wheat flour

Method   Mix the mealie meal and water. Boil for 1 hour and allow to cool till it can be touched. Stir the whole wheat flour into the gruel, cover the container and leave for 24 hours or until the desired degree of sourness is reached. Cool in refrigerator and serve cold.

'Instant' beer

Ingredients   500 g malt starter
                          2 loaves brown bread
                          500 g sugar
                          10 ℓ water
                          2 cubes compressed yeast

Method   Stir everything together. Heat to body temperature and leave to ferment for a few hours. Filter and serve.

This product rather resembles wine in that it has a pink colour and a watery consistency.

Bibliography

Beals, R. L. & Hoijer, H. *An introduction to anthropology.* New York: Macmillan, 1971.

Becker, P. Peoples of southern Africa, their customs and beliefs. *The Star,* 1971.

Beemer, Hilda. Notes on the diet of the Swazi in the Protectorate. *Bantu Studies,* vol. 13, September 1939.

Beemer, Hilda. *The Swazi.* Kimberley: McGregor Museum, 1941.

Böhme, H. F. Some Nguni crafts. *Annals of the South African Museum,* vol. 70, May 1976.

Bruwer, J. P. *Die Bantoe van Suid-Afrika.* Johannesburg: Afrikaanse Pers-Boekhandel, 1963.

Bryant, A. T. *A description of native foodstuffs and their preparation.* Undated booklet.

Bryant, A. T. *Olden times in Zululand and Natal.* Cape Town: Struik, 1965.

Bryant, A. T. *The Zulu people.* Pietermaritzburg: Shuter & Shooter, 1967.

Casalis, E. *The Basuto.* London: Nisbet, 1861.

Coetze, P. J. *Inleiding tot die algemene volkekunde.* Johannesburg: Voortrekkerpers, 1973.

Davison, Patricia & Hosford, June. Lobedu pottery. *Annals of the South African Museum,* vol. 75, June 1978.

Doke, C. M. The earliest records of Bantu. *African Studies,* vol. 19, 1960.

Dornan, S. S. Rainmaking in South Africa. *Bantu Studies,* vol. 3, 1929.

Elliot, Aubrey. *Sons of Zulu.* London/Johannesburg: Collins, 1978.

Elliot, Aubrey. *The magic world of the Xhosa.* London/Johannesburg: Collins, 1975.

Fox, F. W. Some Bantu recipes from the Eastern Cape Province. *Bantu Studies,* vol. 13, 1939.

Fox, F. W. The food value of edible leaves. *South African Medical Journal,* October 1936.

Fox, F. W. Notes on methods of preparation, composition and nutritional value of certain kaffir beers. *Journal of South African Chemical Institute,* vol. 21, 1939.

Gelfund, M. The dietary habits of the African and European with special reference to the Shona-speaking peoples. *South African Medical Journal,* August 1973.

Gelfund, M. *Diet and tradition in an African culture.* London: Livingstone, 1971.

Gitywa, V. Z. The arts and crafts of the Xhosa in the Ciskei: past and present. *Fort Hare Papers,* vol. 5, 1971.

Glukman, M. Zulu women in hoecultural ritual. *Bantu Studies,* vol. 9, 1955.

Gray, Some riddles of the Nyanja people. *Bantu Studies,* vol. 13, 1939.

Hammond-Tooke, W. D. (Ed.) *The Bantu-speaking peoples of southern Africa.* London: Routledge & Kegan Paul, 1974.

Hoff, J. Aletta. *Voedselvoorbereiding en -inname in die tradisionele Tswana-kultuur.* BA(Hons)-studie, Pretoria: UNISA.

Jacot-Guillarmod, A. A contribution towards the economic botany of Basutuland. *Botaniska Notiser*, vol. 119, 1966.

Jones, Sonya M. *A study of Swazi nutrition*. Durban: Institute for Social Research, University of Natal, 1963.

Junod, H. A. *The life of a South African tribe, vols. 1 & 2*. New York: University Books, 1927.

Knuffel, W. E. *The construction of the Bantu grass hut*. Graz: Akademische Druk U Verlagsanstalt, 1973.

Krige, Eileen J. *The social system of the Zulus*. Pietermaritzburg: Shuter & Shooter, 1965.

Kuper, Hilda. *An African aristocracy*. London: Oxford University Press, 1965.

Laubscher, F. X. Origin of mealies. *Farming in South Africa*, April 1944, p. 243.

Lawton, A. C. Bantu pottery of southern Africa. *The Annals of the South African Museum*, vol. 49, 1967.

Lampbrecht, Dora. Basketry in Ngamiland. *Botswana Note and Records*, vol. 8, 1976.

Leary, M. The diet of Pedi school-children. *South African Medical Journal*, vol. 43, 1969.

Lubbe, A. M. A dietary survey in the Mount Ayliff district, Transkei: a preliminary report. *South African Medical Journal*, vol. 47, 1973.

Makeba, Miriam. *The world of African song*. Chicago: Quadrangle, 1971.

Marwick, B. A. *The Swazi*. London: Frank Cass, 1966.

Moning, H. O. *The Pedi*. Pretoria: Van Schaik, 1967.

Murdock, G. P. *Africa: It's people and their cultural history*. London: McGraw-Hill, 1959.

Quinn, P. J. *Foods and feeding habits of the Pedi*. Johannesburg: Witwatersrand University Press, 1959.

Renner, H. D. *The origin of food habits*. London: Faber & Faber, 1944.

Richards, A. I. *Hunger and work in a savage tribe*. London: Routledge, 1932.

Rose, E. F. & Jacot-Guillarmod, A. Plants gathered as foodstuffs by the Transkeian peoples. *South African Medical Journal*, vol. 48, 1974.

Rose, E. F. Some observations on the diet and farming practices of the people of the Transkei. *South African Medical Journal*, vol. 46, 1972.

Schapera, I. *A handbook of Tswana law & custom*. 2nd ed. London: Frank Cass, 1970.

Schapera, I. *The Bantu-speaking tribes of South Africa*. Cape Town: Maskew Miller, 1962.

Schapera, I. *The Tswanas*. London: International African Institute, 1962.

Schoeman, P. J. The Swazi rain ceremony. *Bantu Studies*, vol. 9, 1935.

Shaw, E. Margaret & Van Warmelo, N. J. The material culture of the Cape Nguni. *Annals of the South African Museum*, vol. 58, 1972.

Stayt, H. A. *The Bavenda*. Cass Library of African Studies: General Studies no. 58. London: Frank Cass, 1968.

Stoffberg, D. P. *Die tegniese skeppinge van die Bantwane van die distrik Groblersdal*. Ongepubliseerde MA-verhandeling, Universiteit van Pretoria, 1967.

Soga, J. H. *The Ama-Xosa: life and customs*. Lovedale, CP: Lovedale Press, 1932.

Theal, G. M. *The yellow and dark-skinned people of South Africa*. London: Swan Sonnenschein, 1910.

Van Zyl, H. J. Some of the commonest games played by the Sotho people of the Northern Transvaal. *Bantu Studies*, vol. 13, 1939.

Walton, J. *South African peasant architecture, Nguni folk building*. Johannesburg: Witwatersrand University Press.

West, M. & Morris, Jean. *Abantu*. Cape Town: Struik, 1976.

Wilson, M. Early history of the Transkei and Ciskei. *African Studies*, vol. 18, 1959.

Wilson, M. *Reaction to conquest*. London: Oxford University Press, 1961.

Index of recipes